AGLAONICE

Astronomer and Thaumaturge

PROFILE

Date of Birth
Circa 2nd Century BCE

Place of Birth
Ancient Greece

Date of Death
Unknown

Nationality
Ancient Greece

CAREER

Astronomer and We[...]
Ancient Greece

- Utilized keen obs[...] lunar patterns and celestial events.
- Developed expertise in predicting weather changes based on lunar observations.
- Earned reputation for accurate predictions, particularly related to lunar phenomena.

EDUCATION

Self-taught Astronomer, Greece (circa 2nd century BCE)

CONTRIBUTIONS

- Pioneered the art of lunar prediction and weather forecasting in ancient Greece.
- Elevated the understanding of lunar cycles and their impact on natural events.
- Served as a respected authority in predicting celestial occurrences, influencing ancient Greek society's daily activities and decision-making.

LEGACY AND IMPACT

- Revolutionized understanding of lunar patterns and celestial phenomena prediction.
- Influential in ancient Greek society for weather forecasting based on lunar observation.
- Laid groundwork for future astronomers and weather forecasters.
- Contributed to the development of early Greek astrological practices.

Hypatia of Alexandria

Neoplatonist Philosopher, Astronomer, and Mathematician

Full Name

Hypatia of Alexandria

Date of Birth:

c. 360 CE

Place of Birth

Alexandria, Egypt

Date of Death

March 415 CE

Nationality

Egyptian-Greek

Education

c. 375-385 CE

Studied mathematics, astronomy, and philosophy under her father, Theon of Alexandria, a renowned mathematician.

Career

c. 400-415 CE

Became head of the Platonist school in Alexandria, succeeding her father.

Achievements And Contributions

- Developed and improved methods for solving mathematical and geometric problems.
- Authored several works, including commentaries on the works of mathematicians and philosophers like Diophantus and Ptolemy.
- Promoted the preservation and study of ancient knowledge, particularly works from Greek mathematicians and astronomers.
- Advocated for the importance of reason, logic, and critical thinking in philosophical debates.

Intellectual and Academic Impact

- Hypatia's contributions helped advance mathematics and astronomy during her time.
- She played a crucial role in preserving and passing on the knowledge of ancient Greek thinkers to future generations.

Ann Preston

Physician, Activist, and Educator

Personal Information

Full Name
Ann Preston

Date of Birth
December 1, 1813

Place of Birth
West Grove, Pennsylvania, USA

Date of Death
April 18, 1872

Nationality
American

Education

1835
Graduated from the Female Medical College of Pennsylvania (now Drexel University College of Medicine) as one of its first female students

Career Highlights

c. 1836
Started her medical practice in Philadelphia, Pennsylvania.

1849
Became the first female dean of a medical school when she was appointed Dean of the Woman's Medical College of Pennsylvania.

Contributions and Achievements

Advocate for women's rights and women's access to medical education and healthcare.

Pioneered efforts to promote proper healthcare for women during pregnancy and childbirth.

Co-founded the Female Medical College of Pennsylvania, aiming to provide medical education for women.

Legacy and Impact

Ann Preston's tireless efforts and leadership significantly advanced women's involvement in the medical field.

Her role as the first female dean of a medical school broke barriers and paved the way for other women in academia and medicine.

Preston's commitment to women's health and education continues to inspire and shape medical practice and advocacy.

ADA LOVELACE

Mathematician and Writer

PROFILE

Full Name
Ada Lovelace (née Augusta Ada Byron)

Date of Birth
December 10, 1815

Place of Birth
London, England

Date of Death
November 27, 1852

Nationality
British

EDUCATION

Received private tutoring in mathematics and science from a young age.

c. 1834: Studied mathematics under Augustus De Morgan and Mary Somerville.

CAREER HIGHLIGHTS

- 1833: Charles Babbage, inventor of the Analytical Engine, recognized her mathematical abilities and they began collaborating on the project.
- Co-authored the first algorithm designed to be processed by a machine, making her the world's first computer programmer.
- Advocated the potential of computers beyond simple calculations, foreseeing their use for creating music, art, and scientific simulations.

CONTRIBUTIONS

- Ada Lovelace's work on the Analytical Engine and her notes on Babbage's designs demonstrated the concept of a programmable computer.
- Her insights into computer programming and algorithms laid the foundation for modern computer science.

LEGACY AND IMPACT

- Ada Lovelace is regarded as a pioneer in computer science and a visionary for recognizing the vast potential of computers.
- The computer programming language "Ada" was named in her honor by the U.S. Department of Defense.

Florence Nightingale

Social reformer, Statistician and the Founder of Modern Nursing

Profile

Date of Birth	May 12, 1820
Place of Birth	Florence, Italy
Date of Death	August 13, 1910
Nationality	British

Education

Educated at home, receiving a broad education in literature, history, and mathematics.

Studied nursing informally and gained practical experience by visiting hospitals and nursing homes.

Career

1854: Volunteered as a nurse during the Crimean War, leading a group of nurses to the British military hospital in Scutari (modern-day Istanbul).

Gained recognition as "The Lady with the Lamp" for her tireless and compassionate nursing care to wounded soldiers during the war.

Contributions

Pioneered modern nursing practices and emphasized the significance of hygiene and sanitation in healthcare.

Introduced evidence-based practices in nursing, documenting data on mortality rates and using statistics for healthcare improvement.

Authored numerous influential books and reports, including "Notes on Nursing," which became a foundational nursing text.

Legacy

Florence Nightingale's work revolutionized nursing and elevated its status as a respected profession.
Her emphasis on hygiene and sanitation significantly reduced mortality rates and transformed hospital practices.

ELIZABETH BLACKWELL, M.D

Physician

PROFILE

Date of Birth

February 3, 1821

Place of Birth

Bristol, England

Date of Death

May 31, 1910

Nationality

British-American

EDUCATION

1845

Graduated with a medical degree from Geneva Medical College in New York, becoming the first woman to earn a medical degree in the United States.

CAREER

1857

Founded the New York Infirmary for Women and Children, providing medical care and training for female physicians.

1868

Co-founded the Women's Medical College of the New York Infirmary, a medical school for women.

CONTRIBUTIONS AND ACHIEVEMENTS

Pioneered the way for women in medicine, breaking gender barriers and challenging societal norms.

Advocated for improved healthcare for women and children, emphasizing the importance of female doctors.

LEGACY AND IMPACT

Elizabeth Blackwell's achievement as the first woman to earn a medical degree opened doors for women in the medical profession.

Her efforts to establish medical institutions for women paved the way for the education and training of female physicians.

CLARA BARTON

NURSE AND FOUNDER OF THE AMERICAN RED CROSS

PROFILE

Date of Birth
December 25, 1821

Place of Birth
North Oxford,
Massachusetts, USA

Date of Death
April 12, 1912

Nationality
American

EDUCATION

Educated at home and
attended local schools
in Massachusetts.

CAREER

1854 Became a teacher, later becoming the first
female clerk at the U.S. Patent Office in
Washington, D.C.

1861 Responded to the outbreak of the American
Civil War, providing supplies and medical aid
to soldiers.

1881 Founded the American Red Cross, serving as
its first president.

CONTRIBUTIONS

- Earned the nickname "Angel of the Battlefield" for
her dedicated efforts in providing medical care and
supplies to wounded soldiers during the Civil War.
- Pioneered the concept of battlefield nursing and
established first-aid stations to aid wounded
soldiers.
- Advocated for the establishment of the American
Red Cross and played a pivotal role in its growth
and humanitarian missions.

LEGACY AND IMPACT

- Clara Barton's compassionate and selfless service
during the Civil War revolutionized nursing and
emergency medical care.

REBECCA LEE CRUMPLER

Physician, Nurse and Author

PROFILE

Date of Birth
February 8, 1831

Place of Birth
Delaware, USA

Date of Death
March 9, 1895

Nationality
American

EDUCATION

1852
Graduated from the New England Female Medical College, becoming the first African-American woman to earn a medical degree.

CAREER

- c. 1853: Moved to Boston, Massachusetts, where she practiced as a nurse and doctor.
- Served the medical needs of freed slaves in the South during the American Civil War.

CONTRIBUTIONS AND ACHIEVEMENTS

- Pioneered the path for African-American women in medicine, breaking barriers of race and gender.
- Published "A Book of Medical Discourses" in 1883, becoming one of the first medical publications authored by an African-American.

LEGACY AND IMPACT

- Rebecca Lee Crumpler's achievements in medicine inspired African-American women to pursue careers in healthcare.
- Her dedication to serving underserved communities, particularly freed slaves during the Civil War, left a lasting impact on public health and medicine.

Mary Edwards Walker

Abolitionist, Prohibitionist, Prisoner of War, and Surgeon

Profile

Date of Birth
November 26, 1832

Place of Birth
Oswego, New York, USA

Date of Death
February 21, 1919

Nationality
American

Education

Attended public schools in New York and taught in a one-room schoolhouse before pursuing higher education in medicine.

Career

1855   Graduated with a medical degree from Syracuse Medical College, becoming one of the first female physicians in the United States.

1861   Volunteered as a contract surgeon during the American Civil War, serving on the front lines and in military hospitals.

Contributions and Achievements

Pioneered the path for women in medicine, demonstrating the competence and dedication of female physicians.

As a Civil War surgeon, Walker's bravery and exceptional medical skills earned her the Congressional Medal of Honor in 1865, making her the only woman to receive such an honor.

Legacy and Impact

Her courage and determination as a frontline surgeon during the Civil War left a lasting impact on military medicine and nursing.

Walker's receipt of the Medal of Honor remains a testament to the invaluable contributions of women in times of conflict.

ELIZABETH GARRETT ANDERSON

Physician and Suffragist

PROFILE

Date of Birth
June 9, 1836

Place of Birth
Whitechapel, London, England

Date of Death
December 17, 1917

Nationality
British

EDUCATION

1859
Enrolled at the Middlesex Hospital Medical School in London, becoming the first woman to attend a medical school in the United Kingdom.

CAREER

1865
Became the first woman to qualify as a physician and surgeon in the United Kingdom.

1872
Founded the New Hospital for Women in London, offering medical education and healthcare services for women.

1874
Became the first woman to be added to the British Medical Register, allowing her to practice medicine officially.

CONTRIBUTIONS AND ACHIEVEMENTS

- Pioneered the path for women in medicine, overcoming significant gender-based obstacles and discrimination.
- Championed women's access to medical education and paved the way for other women to enter the medical profession.

LEGACY AND IMPACT

- Elizabeth Garret Anderson's groundbreaking achievements advanced women's rights and opportunities in the medical field.
- Her efforts in establishing the New Hospital for Women provided essential medical services and training for female physicians.

MARGARET E. KNIGHT

INVENTOR

CAREER

c. 1867: Invented a machine for making flat-bottomed paper bags, revolutionizing the paper bag manufacturing industry.

Patented the machine in 1871, becoming one of the first women to hold a patent in the United States.

CONTRIBUTIONS AND ACHIEVEMENTS

Pioneered advancements in paper bag production, making the process more efficient and widely accessible.

Registered multiple patents for various inventions, demonstrating her creativity and engineering skills.

PROFILE

Date of Birth   February 14, 1838

Place of Birth   York, Maine, USA

Date of Death   October 12, 1914

Nationality   American

EDUCATION

No formal education beyond elementary school due to financial constraints.

LEGACY AND IMPACT

Margaret E. Knight's invention of the paper bag machine transformed the packaging industry and improved everyday life for people around the world.

Her success as an inventor and entrepreneur challenged gender norms and inspired other women to pursue careers in engineering and innovation.

PHYSICIAN, TEACHER, SCIENTIST, WRITER, AND SUFFRAGIST

PROFILE

Date of Birth
August 31, 1842

Place of Birth
London, England

Date of Death
June 10, 1906

Nationality
American

EDUCATION

1861 Graduated with honors from the New York Normal College

1864 Earned medical degree from the Woman's Medical College of Pennsylvania.

MARY PUTNAM JACOBI

CAREER

1871
Became the first woman to be admitted to the Ecole de Medecine in Paris, where she completed postgraduate studies.

1876
Became the first woman member of the New York Academy of Medicine.

CONTRIBUTIONS AND ACHIEVEMENTS

Made significant contributions to gynecology and women's health, particularly in the study and treatment of menstrual disorders.

Published numerous research papers and books on medical subjects, including her groundbreaking work on the effects of menstruation on women's health.

LEGACY AND IMPACT

Mary Putnam Jacobi's research and advocacy played a crucial role in advancing women's access to medical education and opportunities in the medical profession.

Her contributions to gynecology and women's health significantly improved medical knowledge and patient care in these fields.

Ogino Ginko
Physician

PROFILE

Full Name
Ogino Ginko (sometimes written as Ginko Ogino)

Date of Birth
October 5, 1851

Place of Birth
Tokyo, Japan

Date of Death
April 21, 1913

Nationality
Japanese

EDUCATION

- In the late 19th century, Ginko Ogino became one of the first Japanese women to study medicine in the United States.

- She attended the Women's Medical College of Pennsylvania (now Drexel University College of Medicine) in Philadelphia, where she pursued her medical education.

CONTRIBUTIONS

- After completing her medical studies, Ogino Ginko returned to Japan, becoming one of the first female doctors in her country.

- As a pioneering woman in medicine, she played a crucial role in breaking gender barriers and promoting women's education and professional advancement.

- Ginko Ogino's work in medicine helped advance healthcare and medical knowledge in Japan, particularly in the field of pathology.

LEGACY AND IMPACT

- Ogino Ginko's determination and dedication to pursuing a career in medicine paved the way for other Japanese women to enter the medical profession.

- She is remembered as a trailblazer for women's rights and gender equality in Japan, inspiring generations of women to pursue higher education and careers in various fields, including medicine.

MARY ANDERSON

REAL ESTATE DEVELOPER, RANCHER, VITICULTURIST, AND INVENTOR

CAREER

c. 1880	Moved to Louisville, Kentucky, and worked as a secretary and stenographer.
1903	Invented the windshield wiper system.

CONTRIBUTIONS AND ACHIEVEMENTS

Patented the first manually operated windshield wiper system, improving visibility and safety for drivers in inclement weather.

Her invention paved the way for the development of automatic windshield wipers, becoming a standard feature in modern vehicles.

LEGACY AND IMPACT

Mary Anderson's invention of the windshield wiper had a profound impact on automotive safety, benefiting drivers and passengers worldwide.

Despite facing challenges and initially limited recognition for her invention, her contributions to automobile technology are now widely acknowledged and celebrated.

PERSONAL INFORMATION

Date of Birth
February 19, 1866

Place of Birth
Greene County, Kentucky, USA

Date of Death
May 29, 1953

Nationality
American

EDUCATION

No formal education beyond elementary school due to family circumstances.

MARIE CURIE

Physicist

Full Name: Marie Curie
(née Maria Skłodowska)

Date of Birth: November 7, 1867

Place of Birth: Warsaw, Poland

Date of Death: July 4, 1934

Nationality: Polish and French

EDUCATION

1883-1889

Graduated with a gold medal from the Gymnasium No. 1, Warsaw, Poland.

1891 - 1893

Obtained a Bachelor of Science degree in Physics, ranked first in her class at the University of Paris (Sorbonne).

1894

Earned a Bachelor of Science degree in Mathematics.

1895

Completed a Master of Science degree in Physics, ranked first in her class again.

1903

Doctorate in Physics from the University of Paris, becoming the first woman to earn a Ph.D. in France.

CAREER

1897 Began research on radioactivity, coining the term "radioactivity" and making pioneering contributions to the field.

1898 Discovered the elements polonium and radium, and coined the term "radioactive" to describe their properties.

1903 Awarded the Nobel Prize in Physics, along with Pierre Curie and Henri Becquerel, for her groundbreaking research on radioactivity.

1906 Appointed as the first female professor at the University of Paris (Sorbonne), where she conducted her research.

1911 Won a second Nobel Prize, this time in Chemistry, in recognition of her discovery and investigation of radium and polonium.

1914 Established the Radium Institute in Paris to further research on radioactivity and its medical applications.

1929 Elected as a member of the International Atomic Weights Committee.

1932 Became a member of the Academy of Medicine.

ALICE HAMILTON

PHYSICIAN, RESEARCH
SCIENTIST, AND AUTHOR

PROFILE

Date of Birth: February 27, 1869

Place of Birth: Fort Wayne,
Indiana, USA

Date of Death: September 22,
1970

Nationality: American

EDUCATION

1893
Graduated from the University of
Michigan Medical School,
becoming one of the first female
medical school graduates.

CAREER

1897   Appointed as an assistant at the new
Johns Hopkins University's Henry Phipps
Institute for Tuberculosis in Baltimore.

1919   Became the first woman faculty member
at Harvard University as an assistant
professor in Industrial Medicine.

CONTRIBUTIONS AND ACHIEVEMENTS

Pioneered the field of occupational medicine,
focusing on the impact of workplace conditions
on workers' health.

Conducted extensive research on industrial
toxicology, occupational diseases, and the health
hazards faced by industrial workers.

Played a vital role in improving workplace safety
and advocating for labor regulations to protect
workers from hazardous conditions.

LEGACY AND IMPACT

Alice Hamilton's pioneering work in occupational
medicine paved the way for modern
occupational health practices.

Her research and advocacy led to significant
improvements in worker safety and health
standards, protecting countless lives.

Vera Gedroits
Doctor of Medicine and Author

Full Name Princess Vera Ignatievna Gedroits
Date of Birth April 19, 1870
Place of Birth Kiev, Russian Empire (now Ukraine)
Date of Death March 20, 1932
Nationality Russian

Education and Career

1890 Graduated with honors from the Smolny Institute in St. Petersburg, Russia.

1892 Enrolled in medical school at the University of Zurich, Switzerland.

1900 Became the first female surgeon in Russia after completing her medical studies.

Contributions and Achievements

- Pioneered surgical techniques and advances in abdominal surgery, particularly in the treatment of appendicitis and gallbladder diseases.
- Developed innovative methods for managing battlefield injuries during World War I, saving numerous lives on the Eastern Front.
- Wrote several medical books and publications, sharing her expertise and contributing to medical education.

Legacy and Impact

- Vera Gedroits' groundbreaking contributions to surgery and battlefield medicine saved countless lives and improved surgical practices.
- As the first female surgeon in Russia, she broke gender barriers and paved the way for other women in medicine.
- Gedroits' legacy as a skilled surgeon and innovative medical researcher continues to be celebrated in the fields of surgery and medical education.

ESTHER PAK

PHYSICIAN

PROFILE

Full Name
Esther Pak (née Kim Jeom-dong)

Date of Birth
March 16, 1876

Place of Birth
Jeong-dong, Seoul, Korea

Date of Death
April 13, 1910

Nationality
Korean

EDUCATION

- Ewha Girls' School, Seoul, Korea
- One-year school in New York (Studied Latin, Physics, and Mathematics)
- Women's Medical College of Baltimore, United States (Graduated in 1900 with a medical degree)

CAREER

- First Korean woman to practice Western medicine in Korea
- Settled in Bogu-yogwan (the first female hospital in Korea) and helped over 3,000 patients
- Worked in the hospital established by Dr. Rosetta Sherwood Hall in Pyongyang
- Traveled across Korea to provide medical care during the cholera epidemic
- Conducted educational and teaching activities, training the first generation of Korean female doctors
- Promoted health education, women's education, and Christianity

Legacy and Impact

- Received a silver medal from Emperor Gojong in 1909
- Featured in the missionary pageant "A Cloud of Witnesses" in 1933
- Inducted into the Korean Science and Technology Hall of Fame by the Korean Academy of Sciences in 2006
- The Ewha University Alumni Committee established the Esther Park Medal in 2008 to recognize women who graduated from the university and became doctors

LISE MEITNER
PHYSICIST

PROFILE

Date of Birth

November 7, 1878

Place of Birth

Vienna, Austria-Hungary (now

Austria)

Date of Death

October 27, 1968

Nationality

Austrian-Swedish

EDUCATION

1901

Received a doctorate in

physics from the University of

Vienna, becoming one of the

first women to earn a Ph.D. in

physics in Austria.

CAREER

1907 Collaborated with Otto Hahn and Fritz Strassmann on radioactivity research, starting a long and influential scientific partnership.

1926 Appointed as the first female physics professor in Germany at the University of Berlin.

CONTRIBUTIONS AND ACHIEVEMENTS

Pioneered the field of nuclear physics, particularly in the study of radioactivity and nuclear fission.

Played a crucial role in discovering and understanding nuclear fission, a groundbreaking development in modern physics.

Her insights and calculations laid the foundation for the work that led to the development of nuclear energy and atomic weapons.

LEGACY AND IMPACT

Lise Meitner's contributions to nuclear physics significantly advanced our understanding of atomic processes and energy.

Her role as a pioneering woman in science inspired future generations of female scientists and broke barriers for women in academia and research.

Meitner's impact on nuclear physics continues to influence scientific research and nuclear technology to this day.

EMMY NOETHER

MATHEMATICIAN

PERSONAL DETAILS

Full Name
Amalie Emmy Noether

Date of Birth
March 23, 1882

Place of Birth
Erlangen, Bavaria, German Empire (now Germany)

Date of Death
April 14, 1935

Nationality
German

EDUCATION

1903
Enrolled at the University of Erlangen, facing barriers as a woman in higher education.

1907
Completed her doctoral dissertation, earning a Ph.D. in mathematics.

CAREER

1915
Joined David Hilbert and Felix Klein at the University of Göttingen as an unpaid lecturer, given recognition as a leading mathematician.

1919
Appointed as an extraordinary professor at the University of Göttingen, becoming the first woman to hold such a position in Germany.

CONTRIBUTIONS AND ACHIEVEMENTS

- Pioneered groundbreaking work in abstract algebra and contributed significantly to the development of modern algebra.

- Formulated Noether's Theorem, establishing a fundamental connection between symmetries in physics and conservation laws.

- Her contributions to theoretical physics and mathematics profoundly influenced the fields of algebra, geometry, and theoretical physics.

LEGACY AND IMPACT

- Emmy Noether's legacy as a brilliant mathematician and physicist continues to shape the fields of mathematics and theoretical physics.

- Despite facing discrimination as a woman in academia, she overcame barriers and earned recognition as one of the most significant mathematicians of her time.

- Noether's work laid the groundwork for further advancements in mathematics and theoretical physics, and her contributions remain celebrated and studied by researchers worldwide.

EDITH CLARKE

ELECTRICAL ENGINEER

Date of Birth: February 10, 1883
Place of Birth: Howard County, Maryland, USA
Date of Death: October 29, 1959
Nationality: American

CONTRIBUTIONS AND ACHIEVEMENTS

- Pioneered advancements in electrical engineering, particularly in power system analysis and electrical transmission.

- Invented the graphical calculator, known as the Clarke calculator, used for solving power transmission line problems.

- Authored numerous technical papers, contributing to the understanding of electrical power transmission.

EDUCATION

1908
Graduated with a degree in mathematics from Vassar College.

1912
Earned a master's degree in electrical engineering from the Massachusetts Institute of Technology (MIT), becoming the first woman to do so.

CAREER

c. 1919
Worked as an electrical engineer and mathematician at General Electric.

1921
Joined the faculty of the Electrical Engineering Department at the University of Texas at Austin.

LEGACY AND IMPACT

- Edith Clarke's contributions to electrical engineering significantly advanced the field and improved power system analysis techniques.

- Her groundbreaking work on the Clarke calculator and power transmission laid the foundation for modern electrical engineering practices.

CHIKA KURODA

Chemist

CAREER

1905 Started her career as a chemist, focusing on research in organic chemistry and natural products.

1909 Returned to Japan after studying in Europe and the United States.

1923 Became the first woman to be appointed as an assistant professor at the University of Tokyo, breaking gender barriers in academia.

1924 Published her landmark research on the structures of natural substances, contributing to the understanding of essential oils and fragrances.

1926 Promoted to the position of full professor, further solidifying her prominent role in the field of chemistry in Japan.

1933 Became the first woman to receive the Chemical Society of Japan Award for her significant contributions to the field.

CONTRIBUTIONS AND ACHIEVEMENTS

- Chika Kuroda's pioneering work in organic chemistry and natural products had a significant impact on the field and inspired future generations of chemists.
- Her research on terpenes and natural substances provided crucial insights into their structures and applications.

PROFILE

Date of Birth: November 12, 1884
Place of Birth: Tokyo, Japan
Date of Death: June 5, 1968
Nationality: Japanese

EDUCATION

- Chika Kuroda studied chemistry at the University of Tokyo, where she earned her bachelor's and master's degrees.
- She later pursued further studies in Europe and the United States, including attending the Sorbonne in Paris, France.

Muthulakshmi Reddy

MEDICAL PRACTITIONER AND SOCIAL REFORMER

 PROFILE

Date of Birth
July 30, 1886

Place of Birth
Pudukkottai, Madras Presidency, British India (now Tamil Nadu, India)

Date of Death
July 22, 1968

Nationality
Indian

 EDUCATION

1912 Muthulakshmi Reddy became one of the first women to graduate with a medical degree in India from Madras Medical College.

 CAREER

1914 Joined the Government Maternity and Ophthalmic Hospital in Chennai as the first female house surgeon.

1918 Became the first woman to work as a doctor in the Women and Children's Hospital in Chennai.

1926 Elected to the Madras Legislative Council, becoming the first woman legislator in British India.

1927 Co-founded the Women's Indian Association (WIA), an organization that advocated for women's rights and social reform.

1930 Was appointed to the Madras University Senate, another significant milestone for a woman in India at that time.

1948 Became the first woman Deputy President of the Legislative Council in Madras.

1956 Reddy was nominated to the Rajya Sabha (the upper house of the Indian Parliament).

Alice Ball

CHEMIST

As one of the first African-American women to receive a master's degree in chemistry, she inspired future generations of women and minorities in science and medicine.

- **Full Name:** Alice Augusta Ball
- **Place of Birth:** Seattle, Washington, USA
- **Nationality:** American

- **Date of Birth:** July 24, 1892
- **Date of Death:** December 31, 1916

EDUCATION AND CAREER

1912

Graduated with a bachelor's degree in pharmaceutical chemistry from the University of Washington, becoming the first woman to do so.

1914

Enrolled in a master's program in chemistry at the University of Hawaii, focusing on the study of chaulmoogra oil for leprosy treatment.

1916

Developed the "Ball Method," a successful technique to extract and isolate the active compounds from chaulmoogra oil.

CONTRIBUTIONS AND ACHIEVEMENTS

- Pioneered groundbreaking research in the treatment of leprosy, offering a more effective approach to manage the disease.
- Her "Ball Method" significantly improved the formulation of chaulmoogra oil, making it more accessible and applicable for leprosy patients.

LEGACY AND IMPACT

- Alice Ball's contributions to leprosy treatment had a profound impact on the lives of many patients, improving their quality of life.
- As one of the first African-American women to receive a master's degree in chemistry, she inspired future generations of women and minorities in science and medicine.

María Orosa

Food Technologist, Pharmaceutical Chemist, and Humanitarian

Profile

Full Name

María Orosa Yñiguez

Date of Birth:

November 29, 1893

Place of Birth

Taal, Batangas, Philippines

Date of Death

March 15, 1945

Nationality

Filipino

Education

Early 1910s	Studied pharmacy at the University of Washington in Seattle, United States.

Career

1922	After completing her studies, Orosa returned to the Philippines and became a registered pharmacist.
1920s and 1930s	María Orosa developed numerous food inventions and formulations, particularly focused on extending the shelf life of traditional Filipino foods.

Achievements And Contributions

- María Orosa is best known for her innovative work in food preservation, which helped address food shortages during World War II.
- She invented the process of creating the "Banana Ketchup," a popular and uniquely Filipino condiment made from bananas, during a shortage of tomatoes.
- Orosa also developed a method of producing "Camote Cue," a sweet snack made from camote (sweet potatoes), to provide an affordable and nutritious food option during difficult times.
- Her research and creations not only preserved traditional Filipino foods but also contributed to the development of the Filipino culinary identity.

Gerty Cori
Biochemist

Profile

Full Name
Gerty Theresa Cori (née Radnitz)

Date of Birth
August 15, 1896

Place of Birth
Prague, Austria-Hungary (now Czech Republic)

Date of Death
October 26, 1957

Nationality
American

Career

1914 Married Carl Ferdinand Cori, with whom she formed a successful scientific partnership.

1931 Appointed as an assistant professor at Washington University in St. Louis, Missouri, where she conducted her groundbreaking research.

Education

1920 Graduated with a medical degree from the German University of Prague.

1924 Earned a doctorate in medicine from the University of Vienna.

Contributions and Achievements

- Pioneered groundbreaking research on carbohydrate metabolism and glycogen storage in the human body.
- Discovered the Cori cycle, a crucial process in the metabolism of glucose and energy production in muscle and liver cells.
- Awarded the Nobel Prize in Physiology or Medicine in 1947, becoming the first American woman to receive the prestigious honor.

Kazue Togasaki

Medical Doctor

PERSONAL INFORMATION

Date of Birth
June 29, 1897

Place of Birth
San Francisco,
California, USA

Date of Death
December 15, 1992

Nationality
Japanese American

EDUCATION

- Bachelor's degree in Zoology from Stanford University
- Registered Nurse (RN) degree from Children's Hospital School of Nursing
- Degree in Public Health from the University of California
- Doctorate of Medicine from Woman's Medical College of Pennsylvania

CAREER

- Worked as a nurse and fundraiser before pursuing a medical degree
- Provided medical services to Japanese detainees during World War II
- Established a medical practice in San Francisco, specializing in obstetrics and gynecology
- Delivered thousands of babies and earned a reputation as a pillar in the Japanese American community
- Treated diverse patients and offered medical care regardless of their ability to pay
- Provided support and care to unwed mothers and terminally ill patients
- Recognized as one of the "Most Distinguished Women of 1970" by the San Francisco Examiner

LEGACY

- One of the earliest women of Japanese ancestry to earn a medical degree in the United States
- Set an example for her siblings, many of whom also pursued careers in medicine
- Remembered for her charitable acts and devotion to medical practice
- Known for her dedication to providing medical services to Japanese detainees during World War II

IRÈNE CURIE

CHEMIST, PHYSICIST AND POLITICIAN

- **Full Name:** Irène Joliot-Curie
- **Date of Birth:** September 12, 1897
- **Place of Birth:** Paris, France
- **Date of Death:** March 17, 1956
- **Nationality:** French

CAREER

1928 Collaborated with her husband, Frédéric Joliot, on groundbreaking research in nuclear physics.

1935 Appointed as a professor at the Faculty of Science in Paris, becoming the first female professor at the institution.

CONTRIBUTIONS AND ACHIEVEMENTS

- Pioneered research in artificial radioactivity, discovering that certain elements could be artificially made radioactive by bombarding them with alpha particles.

- Awarded the Nobel Prize in Chemistry in 1935 with her husband for their discovery of induced radioactivity.

EDUCATION

1925 Graduated with a degree in physics from the University of Paris.

1927 Earned a doctorate in science from the Faculty of Sciences at the University of Paris.

LEGACY AND IMPACT

- Irène Curie's contributions to nuclear physics and radioactivity significantly advanced our understanding of atomic processes.

- Her groundbreaking research on artificial radioactivity opened new avenues for scientific inquiry and medical applications of radioisotopes.

Janaki Ammal Edavalath Kakkat

Botanist

Personal Information

Date of Birth
November 4, 1897

Place of Birth
Tellicherry, Madras
Presidency, British India
(now Kerala, India)

Date of Death
February 7, 1984

Nationality
Indian

Education

1921
Earned Bachelor of Science
degree in botany at the
University of Madras (now
Chennai)

1925
Completed Master's degree
in botany from the
University of Michigan

Career

1930s   Worked as a geneticist and plant
breeder at the Sugarcane Breeding
Institute in Coimbatore, India.

1931   Conducted extensive research on
sugarcane genetics, hybridization, and
crop improvement, leading to the
development of superior sugarcane
varieties.

1951   Worked as the Director of the Central
Botanical Laboratory in Allahabad.

Contributions and Achievements

- Janaki Ammal made significant contributions
to the fields of botany, horticulture, and
agricultural genetics, with a focus on
sugarcane improvement.

- She conducted pioneering research on
sugarcane breeding, which led to the
development of disease-resistant and high-
yielding sugarcane varieties in India.

- Ammal's work in botanical research and
horticulture earned her recognition both
nationally and internationally.

Helen Brooke Taussig

Cardiologist

PROFILE

Full Name
Helen Brooke Taussig

Date of Birth
May 24, 1898

Place of Birth
Cambridge, Massachusetts, USA

Date of Death
May 20, 1986

Nationality
American

EDUCATION

1921
Graduated magna cum laude from Radcliffe College (now part of Harvard University).

1927
Earned a medical degree from the Johns Hopkins School of Medicine, becoming one of the first women to do so.

CAREER

1930 Joined the staff at the Harriet Lane Home for Invalid Children at Johns Hopkins Hospital, where she became interested in pediatric cardiology.

1944 Published a landmark paper on "Congenital Malformations of the Heart," which laid the foundation for modern pediatric cardiology.

CONTRIBUTIONS

- Pioneered the field of pediatric cardiology, focusing on congenital heart defects in children.

- Developed the concept and surgical procedure for the "Blalock-Taussig Shunt," a surgical technique to treat "blue baby" syndrome, now known as Tetralogy of Fallot.

- Played a pivotal role in the development of open-heart surgery for children with congenital heart conditions.

LEGACY AND IMPACT

- Helen Brooke Taussig's contributions to pediatric cardiology revolutionized the treatment of congenital heart defects and saved countless lives.

MARGARET LIN XAVIER

PHYSICIAN

EDUCATION

- Holy Sacred Heart of Jesus Convent, Singapore
- Clark's Commercial College, London
- London School of Medicine for Women and the Royal Free Hospital
- MBBS, MRCS, and LRCP

CAREER

- Obstetrician at Thai Red Cross Society, King Chulalongkorn Memorial Hospital, and Bang Rak medical facility under the Ministry of Public Health
- Established "Unakan" medical clinic with her half sister Chan Xavier

ACHIEVEMENTS AND CONTRIBUTIONS

- First Thai woman to receive a degree in medicine
- Provided medical care to patients of all social classes, including impoverished sex workers whom she treated free of charge
- Highlight of her career: delivering Mom Rajawongse Sirikit Kitiyakara, who would become Queen Sirikit of Thailand

LEGACY

- Remembered for breaking barriers as the first Thai woman in medicine
- Honored for her dedication to providing medical care to the less fortunate and underprivileged

PROFILE

Full Name

Margaret Lin Xavier (Khun Ying Srivisanvaja)

Date of Birth

29 May 1898

Place of Birth

Bangkok, Thailand (then Siam)

Date of Death

6 December 1932

Nationality

Thai

CECILIA PAYNE-GAPOSCHKIN

Astronomer

ABOUT ME

Full Name: Cecilia Helena Payne-Gaposchkin

Date of Birth: May 10, 1900

Place of Birth: Wendover, Buckinghamshire, England

Date of Death: December 7, 1979

Nationality: British-American

EDUCATION

1923: Graduated with first-class honors in physics from Newnham College, University of Cambridge, UK.

1925: Moved to the United States to pursue graduate studies at Harvard College Observatory.

CAREER

1925 Became the first person to earn a Ph.D. in astronomy from Radcliffe College, a division of Harvard University.

1938 Appointed as an assistant professor at Harvard, where she conducted pioneering research in stellar astrophysics.

CONTRIBUTIONS AND ACHIEVEMENTS

- Pioneered groundbreaking research in stellar spectroscopy and astrophysics, particularly on the chemical composition of stars.

- Demonstrated that stars are composed primarily of hydrogen and helium, disproving prevailing theories about stellar composition.

- Published the influential book "Stellar Atmospheres" in 1925, which became a fundamental work in astrophysics.

LEGACY AND IMPACT

- Cecilia Payne-Gaposchkin's research revolutionized our understanding of stellar composition and the structure of stars.

- Her discovery that hydrogen and helium are the primary components of stars laid the foundation for modern astrophysical theories.

BARBARA MCCLINTOCK

SCIENTIST AND CYTOGENETICIST

PROFILE

Date of Birth
June 16, 1902

Place of Birth
Hartford, Connecticut, USA

Date of Death
September 2, 1992

Nationality
American

EDUCATION

1923
Graduated with a bachelor's degree in botany from Cornell University.

1927
Earned a Ph.D. in botany from Cornell University, specializing in cytogenetics.

CAREER

1927-1931 Conducted postdoctoral research at the University of Missouri, where she started her groundbreaking work in genetics.

1941 Joined the staff at Cold Spring Harbor Laboratory in New York, where she spent most of her career.

CONTRIBUTIONS AND ACHIEVEMENTS

- Pioneered the field of cytogenetics and made significant discoveries in the genetics of maize (corn).
- Discovered "jumping genes" or transposable elements, revealing the dynamic nature of genetic information and its ability to move within a genome.
- Awarded the Nobel Prize in Physiology or Medicine in 1983 for her revolutionary discoveries in genetics.

LEGACY AND IMPACT

- Barbara McClintock's groundbreaking research revolutionized the understanding of genetics and the role of transposable elements in shaping genomes.
- Her discoveries, initially met with skepticism, are now fundamental to modern genetics and molecular biology.

FAHIRE BATTALGIL

Ichthyologist

PROFILE

Full Name
Fahire Akim Hanim

Date of Birth
1902

Place of Birth
Istanbul, Turkey

Date of Death
February 20, 1948

EDUCATION

- Attended the French school of Notre Dame de Sion in Damascus, where her father had also studied
- Graduated from Bezmi Alem High School in 1924
- Obtained a qualification in Natural Science from Darülfünun in 1926
- Pursued further education and earned a master's degree in physics from the University of Maryland

EDUCATION

- Appointed as an Associate Professor of Zoology at the University of Istanbul in 1933 after the reform of Turkish universities
- Participated in expeditions organized by the Fisheries Institute
- Translated lectures of Professor Andre Naville and took over his lectures after his sudden death in 1937
- Became a full Associate Professor in 1937 under the guidance of German Zoologist Curt Kosswig and later a full professor in 1944
- Discovered and described several new fish species for Turkey, including Alburnus adanensis, Barbus oligolepis, Pseudophoxinus caralis, and Squalius cephaloides
- Several fish species were named in her honor, such as Cobitis fahireae, Phoxinellus fahirae, and Alburnus battalgilae

LEGACY

- Pioneering figure in Turkish ichthyology, contributing to the understanding of freshwater fish species in Turkey
- One of the first women to become a professor at a Turkish university

Grace Hopper

Computer Scientist, Mathematician, and United States Navy Rear Admiral

PERSONAL INFORMATION

Full Name
Grace Brewster Murray Hopper

Date of Birth
December 9, 1906

Place of Birth
New York City, New York, USA

Date of Death
January 1, 1992

Nationality
American

EDUCATION

- 1928: Graduated Phi Beta Kappa with a bachelor's degree in mathematics and physics from Vassar College.
- 1934: Earned a master's degree in mathematics from Yale University.
- 1937: Completed her Ph.D. in mathematics from Yale University, becoming one of the first women to earn a Ph.D. in mathematics.

CAREER

- 1943: Joined the United States Navy Reserve (WAVES) during World War II, serving as a commissioned officer.

- 1944: Assigned to work on the Harvard Mark I computer, where she became one of the first programmers of the electro-mechanical computer.

CONTRIBUTIONS AND ACHIEVEMENTS

- Pioneered computer programming and developed the first compiler, known as A-0, which translated instructions into machine code.

- Coined the term "debugging" after removing a moth from a computer, an incident that gave rise to the term for fixing errors in software.

- Contributed significantly to the development of COBOL, one of the first high-level programming languages.

LEGACY AND IMPACT

- Grace Hopper's contributions to computer programming and software development were transformative, laying the groundwork for modern computing.

PROFILE

Date of Birth
June 28, 1906

Place of Birth
Kattowitz, German Empire (now Katowice, Poland)

Date of Death
February 20, 1972

Nationality
German-American

EDUCATION

1930
Earned a Ph.D. in physics from the University of Göttingen, becoming one of the first women to receive a doctorate in physics in Germany.

MARIA GOEPPERT MAYER

THEORETICAL PHYSICIST

CAREER

1930S Faced challenges in securing academic positions due to gender bias, but continued her research independently.

1942-1945 Joined the Manhattan Project during World War II, working on the development of the atomic bomb.

Contributions and Achievements

- Pioneered groundbreaking research in nuclear physics and theoretical chemistry, focusing on the structure of atomic nuclei.
- Formulated the nuclear shell model, a fundamental theory that explained the structure and behavior of atomic nuclei.
- Awarded the Nobel Prize in Physics in 1963, becoming the second woman to receive the Nobel Prize in Physics.

Legacy and Impact

- Maria Goeppert Mayer's research in nuclear physics and her nuclear shell model significantly advanced our understanding of atomic nuclei.
- Her work laid the foundation for modern nuclear physics and continues to be fundamental in the field of nuclear structure.

Personal Information

Date of Birth
September 24, 1907

Place of Birth
Baliuag, Bulacan, Philippines

Date of Death
November 8, 1999

Nationality
Filipino

Education

- **1929:** Earned her Bachelor of Science in Education from the University of the Philippines

- Pursued further studies in chemistry and earned her Master's degree in Chemistry from the University of Michigan in the United States.

Luz Oliveros-Belardo

Chemist

Career Highlights

1930s
Served as a chemistry instructor at the University of the Philippines.

1940s
Became a member of the USAFFE (United States Armed Forces in the Far East) and actively contributed to the Philippine resistance movement against the Japanese occupation during World War II.

After World War II
Worked as a researcher and scientist at the Forest Products Research Institute and the Philippine Science High School.

Contributions and Achievements

Luz Oliveros-Belardo was a renowned scientist and educator, known for her contributions to the field of chemistry and her dedication to scientific research and education in the Philippines.

She conducted research on local Philippine plants and their potential medicinal and practical applications.

Her work on the chemical composition of indigenous Philippine plants contributed to the development of herbal medicines and various useful products.

RACHEL CARSON

Marine Biologist, Writer, and Conservationist

PROFILE

Full Name
Rachel Louise Carson

Date of Birth
May 27, 1907

Place of Birth
Springdale, Pennsylvania, USA

Date of Death
April 14, 1964

Nationality
American

EDUCATION

1929
Graduated magna cum laude with a bachelor's degree in biology from the Pennsylvania College for Women (now Chatham University).

1932
Earned a master's degree in zoology from Johns Hopkins University.

CAREER

1936 Joined the U.S. Bureau of Fisheries (later the U.S. Fish and Wildlife Service), where she began her writing career.

1951 Published "The Sea Around Us," a bestselling book that brought her widespread acclaim.

CONTRIBUTIONS AND ACHIEVEMENTS

- Pioneered environmental conservation and raised public awareness about the impact of human activities on the environment.

- Wrote the seminal book "Silent Spring" in 1962, which exposed the harmful effects of pesticides, particularly DDT, on the environment and wildlife.

- Inspired the modern environmental movement and prompted significant changes in environmental policies and regulations.

CONTRIBUTIONS AND ACHIEVEMENTS

- "Silent Spring" led to the ban of DDT in the United States and sparked the establishment of the U.S. Environmental Protection Agency (EPA).

VIRGINIA APGAR, M.D.

PHYSICIAN, OBSTETRICAL ANESTHESIOLOGIST AND MEDICAL RESEARCHER

PROFILE

Date of Birth
June 7, 1909

Place of Birth
Westfield, New Jersey, USA

Date of Death
August 7, 1974

Nationality
American

EDUCATION

1929
Graduated from Mount Holyoke College with a bachelor's degree in zoology.

1933
Earned a medical degree from the College of Physicians and Surgeons at Columbia University.

CAREER

1938-1949
Worked as a surgical resident and anesthesiologist at Presbyterian Hospital (now NewYork-Presbyterian Hospital).

1949
Developed the Apgar Score, a pioneering system for evaluating the health of newborns shortly after birth.

CONTRIBUTIONS

- Pioneered research in obstetrical anesthesia and made significant contributions to the field of perinatology.
- Created the Apgar Score, a simple and effective method to assess the newborn's health based on five vital signs: Appearance, Pulse, Grimace, Activity, and Respiration.
- The Apgar Score became a global standard for assessing newborns' health and has saved countless lives by identifying babies in need of immediate medical attention.

LEGACY AND IMPACT

- Virginia Apgar's work in obstetrical anesthesia and the development of the Apgar Score have had a lasting impact on neonatal care and infant health.
- Her contributions to perinatology and newborn assessment continue to be fundamental in modern medical practices.

RITA LEVI-MONTALCINI

NEUROBIOLOGIST & FORMER SENATOR OF THE ITALIAN REPUBLIC

PERSONAL INFORMATION

Date of Birth: April 22, 1909

Date of Death: December 30, 2012

Place of Birth: Turin, Italy

Nationality: Italian

EDUCATION

1936
Graduated with a degree in medicine and surgery from the University of Turin, Italy.

1938
Specialized in neurology and psychiatry, obtaining a postgraduate degree in the same field.

CAREER

1940s
Conducted pioneering research on the growth of nerve cells, facing challenges due to World War II and gender bias.

1952
Discovered nerve growth factor (NGF), a crucial protein that stimulates nerve cell growth and survival.

CONTRIBUTIONS

- Pioneered groundbreaking research in neuroscience, particularly on nerve cell development and growth factors.
- Her discovery of NGF revolutionized the understanding of nerve cell biology and its implications in neurodevelopment and neurodegenerative diseases.
- Awarded the Nobel Prize in Physiology or Medicine in 1986, becoming the first woman to receive the Nobel Prize in Medicine.

LEGACY AND IMPACT

- Rita Levi-Montalcini's research in neuroscience significantly advanced our understanding of nerve cell development and neurotrophic factors.
- Her work laid the foundation for the study of growth factors in neurobiology and their potential applications in neurodegenerative disease treatments.

TOSHIKO YUASA

NUCLEAR PHYSICIST

PROFILE

Date of Birth
December 11, 1909

Place of Birth
Taitō Ward, Tokyo

Date of Death
February 1, 1980

Nationality
Japanese

EDUCATION

1927 – 1931
Tokyo Women's Higher Normal School (now Ochanomizu University), Division of Science

1931 – 1934
Tokyo Bunrika University (now the University of Tsukuba), Department of Physics

1943
Doctorate in Science from Collège de France

1962
Doctorate in Science from Kyoto University

CAREER AND CONTRIBUTION

Early Career and Study under Frédéric Joliot-Curie

- Gained recognition as Japan's first female physicist, challenging gender barriers in the field.
- Traveled to Paris, France, to study under Frédéric Joliot-Curie, one of the most eminent physicists of the time.

Pioneering Work in Nuclear Physics

- Conducted groundbreaking research in nuclear physics, contributing to the understanding of atomic nuclei.
- Made significant discoveries in the field of radioactivity and nuclear reactions.

LEGACY

- Awarded the Medal with Purple Ribbon from the Japanese government, 1976

- Posthumously conferred the Order of the Precious Crown of the Third Class, 1980

- Ochanomizu University established the Toshiko Yuasa Prize in 2002 to support young women scientists for further study in France

- Fondly remembered as "the Japanese Madame Curie," inspiring generations of women to pursue careers in STEM.

Fe Villanueva del Mundo

Pediatrician

PROFILE

Date of Birth
November 27, 1911

Place of Birth
Iloilo City, Philippines

Date of Death
June 6, 2011

Nationality
Filipino

EDUCATION

1935
Studied medicine at the University of the Philippines College of Medicine, where she earned her medical degree.

LEGACY

- Dr. Fe Villanueva del Mundo's legacy is marked by her dedication to improving children's health and well-being in the Philippines.

CAREER

1935
Began her medical career as a pediatrician and general practitioner in the Philippines.

1942-1945
Served as a volunteer doctor for the Philippine Red Cross during World War II and provided medical care to prisoners and civilians affected by the war.

1946
Went to the United States for further medical training and specialization in pediatrics and infectious diseases at Harvard Medical School.

CONTRIBUTIONS

- Dr. Fe Villanueva del Mundo is celebrated for her groundbreaking work in pediatrics and child healthcare in the Philippines.

- She introduced the first incubator for premature babies in the Philippines, significantly reducing infant mortality rates.

- Del Mundo established the first pediatric hospital in the Philippines, the Children's Medical Center, which later became the Fe Del Mundo Medical Center in her honor.

DOROTHY CROWFOOT HODGKIN

Chemist

CAREER

1934-1937   Conducted research on X-ray crystallography at the University of Cambridge under J.D. Bernal.

1943-1949   Worked on penicillin research during World War II at the Radcliffe Infirmary in Oxford.

1956   Determined the structure of vitamin B12, a landmark achievement in the field of biochemistry.

CONTRIBUTIONS AND ACHIEVEMENTS

- Pioneered the field of X-ray crystallography and applied it to determine the structures of complex molecules.
- Made groundbreaking contributions to the study of proteins, peptides, and important biomolecules like insulin and vitamin B12.
- Awarded the Nobel Prize in Chemistry in 1964 for her work on the structure of vitamin B12.

LEGACY AND IMPACT

- Dorothy Crowfoot Hodgkin's work in X-ray crystallography revolutionized the study of biomolecular structures.
- Her determination of vitamin B12's structure opened new avenues for understanding the role of essential biomolecules in health and disease.

PROFILE

Full Name: Dorothy Mary Crowfoot Hodgkin
Date of Birth: May 12, 1910
Place of Birth: Cairo, Egypt
Date of Death: July 29, 1994
Nationality: British

EDUCATION

1928   Enrolled at Somerville College, Oxford, to study chemistry.

1932   Graduated with a first-class degree in chemistry from the University of Oxford.

Tsai-Fan Yu
Physician and Researcher

PROFILE

Date of Birth
1911

Place of Birth
Shanghai, China

Date of Death
March 2, 2007

Nationality
Chinese-American

EDUCATION

- Overcame adversity after her mother's death at age 13, with her father's support, to pursue her educational dreams
- Enrolled at Ginling College in China and later admitted to Peking Union Medical College on full scholarship
- Graduated with highest honors and became the Chief Resident in Internal Medicine at Peking Union Medical College in 1939

CAREER

- Conducted research on diseases in citrus fruits and beans while in China
- Migrated to New York in 1947 and became a U.S. citizen in 1950
- Taught at Columbia University College of Physicians and Surgeons before joining Mount Sinai Medical Center in 1957
- Became the first female full professor at Mount Sinai Hospital in 1973

CONTRIBUTIONS

- Discovered the drug probenecid, which facilitated the removal of excess uric acid from the body by promoting its excretion through urine. This marked a major breakthrough in gout treatment, providing relief to countless patients.
- Identified and studied the drug allopurinol as a secondary treatment for gout and an effective method for treating kidney stones.

RECOGNITIONS

- Dr. Yu's exceptional contributions to the field of rheumatology earned her the Distinguished Career Achievement Award from the American Association of Rheumatology.
- She was also honored with the Master Award by the same association, highlighting her immense impact on diagnosing and treating rheumatoid arthritis.

MAGGIE LIM

Physician and Public Health Official

PROFILE

Date of Birth
January 5, 1913
(Maggie Tan)

Place of Birth
Singapore

Date of Death
November 1995

Nationality
Singaporean

EDUCATION

Dr. Lim pursued her passion for medicine and earned her medical degree at the London School of Medicine for Women and the Royal Free Hospital. She returned to Singapore In 1940, ready to make a difference in the healthcare landscape.

CAREER AND CONTRIBUTIONS

- During World War II, Dr. Lim served as a camp doctor at Endau Settlement in Johor, supporting the Malayan Peoples' Anti-Japanese Army.
- After the war, Dr. Lim became an obstetrician and public health official in Singapore.
- Dr. Lim was an honorary medical officer of the Singapore Family Planning Association when it began in 1949.
- Despite facing challenges, including brief detention on charges of spreading Malayan Communist Party propaganda, she continued to contribute to healthcare and maternal and child welfare in Singapore.
- In 1963, she became the head of the maternal and child welfare department in the Ministry of Health, solidifying her position as a leading figure in public health initiatives.
- Dr. Lim served as president of the Family Planning and Population Board and an advisor to the Midwives' Council.
- Later in her career, she became a professor of epidemiology and public health at the University of Hawai'i's East–West Center, making her mark internationally.

CHIEN-SHIUNG WU

Particle and Experimental Physicist

PROFILE

Full Name
Chien-Shiung Wu (also known as Tsien Hsue-shen)

Date of Birth
May 31, 1912

Place of Birth
Liuhe, Jiangsu, China

Date of Death
February 16, 1997

Nationality
Chinese-American

EDUCATION

1936
Earned a bachelor's degree in physics from the National Central University in Nanjing, China.

1940
Obtained a master's degree in physics from the Zhejiang University in Hangzhou, China.

CAREER

1940s   Emigrated to the United States to pursue further education and research opportunities.

1944   Joined the Manhattan Project during World War II, working on the development of the atomic bomb.

1948   Joined the faculty at Columbia University, where she conducted groundbreaking research in beta decay and weak interaction physics.

CONTRIBUTIONS AND ACHIEVEMENTS

- Pioneered significant research in beta decay, conducting experiments that challenged the prevailing belief in the conservation of parity.
- Her "Wu Experiment" in 1956 demonstrated the violation of parity conservation in weak interactions, leading to a Nobel Prize in Physics for her colleagues.
- Played a crucial role in disproving the principle of parity conservation and advancing the understanding of fundamental forces in nature.

KAMALA SOHONIE
Biochemist

PROFILE

Date of Birth
March 14, 1912

Place of Birth
Bombay, British India
(now Mumbai, India)

Date of Death
June 28, 1998

Nationality
Indian

EDUCATION

1932
became one of the first women to graduate with a degree in chemistry from the University of Bombay (now University of Mumbai)

> CAREER

- After completing her undergraduate studies, Kamala Sohonie joined the Indian Institute of Science in Bangalore to continue her education in biochemistry.

- She went to the United States to further her studies and research, where she was admitted to the University of Michigan in Ann Arbor.

> CONTRIBUTIONS AND ACHIEVEMENTS

- Kamala Sohonie's research in biochemistry focused on enzyme kinetics, particularly the study of enzymes that break down carbohydrates in the body.

- She conducted groundbreaking research on pancreatic enzymes and contributed to the understanding of the digestion process.

- Sohonie's work in enzyme kinetics earned her recognition in the scientific community, both in India and internationally.

BIBHA CHOWDHURI

PHYSICIST

PROFILE

Date of Birth
July 3, 1913

Place of Birth
Kolkata, India

Date of Death
June 2, 1991

Nationality
Indian

EDUCATION

- Bibha Chowdhuri earned her MSc in Physics from the University of Calcutta in 1936, where she began her research work into cosmic rays under the guidance of Dr. Bose.

- She went on to pursue a Ph.D. in physics.

CAREER

- Bibha Chowdhuri conducted pioneering research on particle physics and cosmic rays.
- As particle accelerators were not available at the time, she traveled to the tops of mountains to study subatomic particles in cosmic rays using cloud chambers.
- During the late 1930s and early 1940s, Chowdhuri observed a new particle: mesons, and she published her findings in Nature alongside Dr. Bose.
- Due to World War II, she faced challenges in continuing her research.

CONTRIBUTIONS AND ACHIEVEMENTS

- Bibha Chowdhuri made significant contributions to the study of cosmic rays and particle physics, particularly in the discovery of mesons.
- She became the first Indian woman to earn a Ph.D. in physics, cementing her place as a trailblazer in the field.

LEGACY

- The International Astronomical Union re-christened the yellow-white dwarf star HD86081 as "Bibha" in her honor, acknowledging her significant contributions to the field of physics.

Hedy Lamarr

ABOUT ME

Full Name
Hedy Lamarr (Born Hedwig
Eva Maria Kiesler)

Date of Birth
November 9, 1914

Place of Birth
Vienna, Austria-Hungary (now
Austria)

Date of Death
January 19, 2000

Nationality
Austrian-American

EDUCATION

1933 Enrolled at the Max
Reinhardt Theatre School in
Vienna, pursuing her
passion for acting.

CAREER

1938
Moved to Hollywood, California, and
signed a contract with Metro-Goldwyn-
Mayer (MGM), starting her successful
career in Hollywood films.

1940s-1950s
Starred in several successful movies,
becoming one of the most popular and
glamorous actresses of her time.

1942
Co-invented a frequency-hopping spread
spectrum communication system during
World War II, which laid the groundwork
for modern Wi-Fi and Bluetooth
technologies.

1962
Received the Pioneer Award from the
Electronic Frontier Foundation in
recognition of her groundbreaking work
in frequency-hopping spread spectrum
technology.

HISAKO KOYAMA

Astronomer

SUMMARY

Hisako Koyama (小山寿子, 1916 - 1997) was a Japanese astronomer known for her work in sunspot observation and discovery. She became the first woman to be granted a doctorate in astronomy in Japan and made significant contributions to solar physics during her career.

SCIENTIFIC CAREER

- Koyama's early work focused on sunspot observation, and she became an expert in the field of solar physics.
- She made numerous contributions to understanding solar phenomena and the behavior of sunspots.
- Koyama's most significant achievement came in 1946 when she discovered a new type of sunspot, now known as "asymmetrical sunspots" or "Koyama sunspots."
- Her groundbreaking discovery was widely recognized and led to her becoming the first woman to receive a doctorate in astronomy in Japan.

LEGACY

- Hisako Koyama's pioneering work in solar physics and her breakthrough discovery of asymmetrical sunspots significantly advanced the field of astronomy in Japan and globally.
- She inspired other women to pursue careers in astronomy and science, despite the prevailing gender barriers in her time.

EDUCATION

- Despite facing societal and gender barriers, she pursued her passion for astronomy and attended the University of Tokyo to study the subject.

JOAN CLARKE

CRYPTANALYST AND NUMISMATIST

PROFILE

- **Full Name:** Joan Elisabeth Lowther Clarke
- **Date of Birth:** June 24, 1917
- **Place of Birth:** West Norwood, London, England
- **Date of Death:** September 4, 1996
- **Nationality:** British

EDUCATION

1936

Graduated with first-class honors in mathematics from Newnham College, University of Cambridge.

CONTRIBUTIONS

- Pioneered codebreaking and cryptographic work during World War II, contributing significantly to the Allied war effort.
- Played a vital role in decrypting German military communications and enabling crucial intelligence gathering.
- Made invaluable contributions to breaking Enigma-encrypted messages and decoding the Lorenz cipher used by the German High Command.

CAREER

1940 Joined the Government Code and Cypher School (GC&CS) at Bletchley Park during World War II.

1944 Worked closely with Alan Turing and others on the successful decryption of German Enigma messages.

LEGACY AND IMPACT

- Joan Clarke's codebreaking work at Bletchley Park had a profound impact on the outcome of World War II and contributed to the Allied victory.
- Despite facing gender discrimination during her time, Clarke's talent and intelligence were recognized, and she became an integral member of the codebreaking team.

ASIMA CHATTERJEE

ORGANIC CHEMIST

- **Date of Birth:** September 23, 1917
- **Place of Birth:** Bengal, British India (now West Bengal, India)
- **Date of Death:** November 22, 2006
- **Nationality:** Indian

EDUCATION

1944 Ph.D. in Organic Chemistry, University of Calcutta, India

1938 M.Sc. in Chemistry, University of Calcutta, India

1936 B.Sc. with Honors in Chemistry, Scottish Church College, University of Calcutta, India

ACHIEVEMENTS

- Pioneered research on the chemistry of medicinal plants and natural products.

- Discovered anti-epileptic and anti-malarial drugs from Indian medicinal plants.

- Developed anti-inflammatory drugs with potential therapeutic applications.

- First Indian woman to earn a Doctorate in Science from an Indian university.

CAREER

1944-1982 Researcher and Faculty, University of Calcutta, India

1940-1944 Guest Lecturer, Lady Brabourne College, Kolkata, India

LEGACY AND IMPACT

- Broke gender barriers and inspired generations of women to pursue careers in science.

- Received national recognition with awards such as Padma Bhushan and Shanti Swarup Bhatnagar Award.

- Her work has been acclaimed globally, leading to collaborations with international scientists.

- Continues to inspire researchers, especially women, to achieve excellence in scientific endeavors.

Irene Uchida
Scientist, Geneticist and Researcher

Personal Information

Full Name: Irene Ayako Uchida

Date of Birth: April 8, 1917

Date of Death: July 30, 2013

Place of Birth: Vancouver, Canada

Nationality: Canada

Education

- Ph.D. in Zoology, University of Toronto, Canada
- B.A. in English Literature, University of British Columbia, Canada

Career Achievements and Contributions

Groundbreaking Research in Down Syndrome

- Conducted pioneering studies on children with Down syndrome, unraveling the genetic basis of this common birth abnormality.
- Investigated the cause of the extra chromosome in Down syndrome, contributing significantly to the field of cytogenetics.

Investigation of Chromosomal Birth Defects

- Conducted research on the link between abdominal X-rays in pregnant women and chromosomal birth defects.
- Provided evidence that extensive maternal radiation exposure led to increased risk of birth defects in offspring.

Academic and Professional Leadership

- fostering collaboration and knowledge exchange.
- Held advisory roles in esteemed institutions, including the Science Council of Canada and the Canadian College of Medical Geneticists.

Legacy and Impact

- Irene Uchida's work in cytogenetics remains foundational in understanding genetic disorders and chromosomal abnormalities.
- Her groundbreaking research on Down syndrome has paved the way for advancements in medical science and genetic counseling.

THE ENIAC WOMEN

Mathematicians and Programmers

MEMBERS

Betty Jennings Bartik
December 27, 1924 - March 23, 2011

Frances "Fran" Bilas Spence
March 2, 1922 - September 9, 2012

Kathleen McNulty Mauchly Antonelli
February 12, 1921 - April 20, 2006

Marlyn Wescoff Meltzer
May 2, 1922 - December 3, 2008

Ruth Lichterman Teitelbaum
March 28, 1924 - Death: April 6, 1986

Frances "Betty" Holberton
March 7, 1917 - December 8, 2001

BACKGROUND

- During World War II, the U.S. Army commissioned the development of the Electronic Numerical Integrator and Computer (ENIAC) to calculate artillery firing tables.
- The women were recruited as "computers" to manually perform complex mathematical calculations for ballistics.

CONTRIBUTIONS

- Programmed the ENIAC, using plugboards and switches to set up its calculations.
- Played a key role in solving mathematical problems related to ballistics, atomic energy, and other scientific research.
- Developed new methods and techniques for programming and operating the ENIAC.

LEGACY AND IMPACT

- Pioneered the field of computer programming and became some of the first computer programmers in history.
- Their work on the ENIAC laid the foundation for modern computer programming and contributed to the development of subsequent computers.
- Their contributions were largely unrecognized for decades, but efforts have been made to highlight and celebrate their groundbreaking work in recent years.
- In 1997, they were collectively inducted into the Women in Technology International (WITI) Hall of Fame to honor their pioneering achievements.

Gertrude Belle Elion

BIOCHEMIST AND PHARMACOLOGIST

PROFILE

Date of Birth
January 23, 1918

Place of Birth
New York City, New York, USA

Date of Death
February 21, 1999

Nationality
American

EDUCATION

- **1937**: Graduated with a bachelor's degree in chemistry from Hunter College.

- **1941**: Earned a master's degree in chemistry from New York University.

CAREER

1944 Joined the Burroughs Wellcome pharmaceutical company (later GlaxoSmithKline) as a research chemist.

1967 Appointed Head of the Department of Experimental Therapy, becoming the company's first female department head.

CONTRIBUTIONS

- Pioneered the development of numerous life-saving drugs, particularly in the fields of antiviral and anticancer medications.
- Co-invented the first successful antiviral drug, acyclovir, used to treat herpes infections.
- Contributed to the development of medications for organ transplant patients and treatments for leukemia and gout.

LEGACY AND IMPACT

- Gertrude Belle Elion's groundbreaking research in pharmaceuticals significantly improved medical treatments and saved countless lives.

LIN LANYING

ELECTRICAL ENGINEER, MATERIALS SCIENTIST, PHYSICIST, AND POLITICIAN

PROFILE

Date of Birth
February 7, 1918

Place of Birth
Putian, Fujian, China

Date of Death
March 4, 2003

Nationality
Chinese

EDUCATION

1931
Bachelor's Degree in Mathematics
Dickinson College, USA

1938
Bachelor's Degree in Physics
Fukien Christian University

1955
Doctorate Degree in Solid-State Physics
University of Pennsylvania, USA

CAREER

1955	Senior Engineer - Sylvania Company, USA
1957	Researcher - Institute of Physics, Chinese Academy of Sciences (CAS)
	Researcher - Institute of Semiconductor, CAS

Achievements

- Manufactured China's first monocrystalline silicon
- Designed China's first mono-crystal furnace for silicon extraction
- Pioneered developments in microelectronics and optoelectronics
- Conducted groundbreaking research in gallium arsenide, including successful experiments for artificial satellites
- Made significant contributions to semiconductor lasers and integrated circuits

Legacy and Impact

- Lin Lanying is known as the "mother of aerospace materials" and the "mother of semiconductor materials" in China.
- Her pioneering research and dedication to technological advancements have left a lasting impact on China's aerospace and semiconductor industries.

ANNA MANI
PHYSICIST AND METEOROLOGIST

PROFILE

Full Name
Anna Modayil Mani

Date of Birth
23 August 1918

Place of Birth
Peermade, Travancore (now Kerala), India

Date of Death
16 August 2001

Nationality
Indian

EDUCATION

B.Sc Honors degree in Physics and Chemistry
Pachaiyappas College, Chennai (1939)

Scholarship for research
The Indian Institute of Science, Bangalore (1940)

Specialization in Meteorological Instruments
Imperial College, London (1945)

CAREER

- Worked under Prof. C V Raman, conducting research on optical properties of ruby and diamond

- Joined the meteorology department in Pune, published numerous research papers on meteorological instrumentation

- Standardized drawings of nearly one hundred weather instruments to make India independent in weather instruments

- Set up a network of stations to measure solar radiation (1957-1958)

- Established a small workshop in Bangalore for manufacturing wind speed and solar energy instruments

- Worked on developing an apparatus to measure ozone and became a member of the International Ozone Association

- Set up a meteorological observatory and instrumentation tower at the Thumba rocket launching facility

- Associated with scientific organizations including the Indian National Science Academy, American Meteorological Society, and World Meteorological Organization

- Appointed as a WMO consultant in Egypt (1975)

- Transferred to Delhi as the Deputy Director General of the Indian Meteorological Department (1969)

- Retired as Deputy Director General in 1976

KATHERINE G. JOHNSON

MATHEMATICIAN

PERSONAL INFORMATION

Full Name

Katherine Coleman Goble Johnson

Date of Birth

August 26, 1918

Place of Birth

West Virginia, USA

Date of Death

February 24, 2020

Nationality

American

EDUCATION

1937

Graduated summa cum laude with degrees in mathematics and French from West Virginia State College.

CAREER

1937 Joined the National Advisory Committee for Aeronautics (NACA), which later became NASA.

1962 Calculated the trajectory for the first American human spaceflight by astronaut Alan Shepard.

1969 Worked on the calculations for the Apollo 11 mission, which successfully landed humans on the moon.

CONTRIBUTIONS AND ACHIEVEMENTS

- Pioneered essential calculations for NASA's space missions, playing a critical role in the success of early space exploration.

- Provided vital mathematical support to the Mercury, Gemini, and Apollo programs, ensuring precise trajectories and safe spaceflights.

- Overcame gender and racial barriers, becoming a trailblazer for African-American women in science and engineering.

PROFILE

Date of Birth

June 20, 1919

Place of Birth

Hana, Maui, Hawaii, USA

Date of Death

October 28, 2010

Nationality

American

EDUCATION

Bachelor of Arts (Botany)

University of Hawaii at Manoa

1941

Master of Arts (Botany)

University of California, Berkeley

1950

Ph.D. (Botany)

University of California, Berkeley

1952

ISABELLA AIONA ABBOTT

EDUCATOR, PHYCOLOGIST, AND ETHNOBOTANIST

CAREER

1950-1952	Researcher, Stanford University
1952-1954	Assistant Professor, Stanford University
1954-1972	Research Associate, Hopkins Marine Station of Stanford University
1972-1976	Associate Professor, Stanford University
1976-1982	Professor, Stanford University
1982-2010	Professor Emerita, Stanford University

NOTABLE ACHIEVEMENTS

- Pioneered research on marine algae and became a world-renowned expert in the field.
- Discovered and described over 200 species of marine algae, many of them previously unknown to science.
- First woman and first person of Hawaiian ancestry to earn a Ph.D. in science from the University of California, Berkeley.
- Played a significant role in documenting and preserving traditional Hawaiian knowledge of marine algae and their uses in Hawaiian culture.
- Authored numerous scientific papers and books, including "La'au Hawai'i: Traditional Hawaiian Uses of Plants" and "Limu: An Ethnobotanical Study of Some Hawaiian Seaweeds."
- Received multiple awards and honors, including the Gilbert Morgan Smith Medal from the National Academy of Sciences and the Order of the Precious Crown from the Emperor of Japan.
- Advocate for the conservation of marine ecosystems and Hawaiian culture.

Katsuko Saruhashi

Geochemist

PROFILE

Date of Birth
March 22, 1920

Place of Birth
Tokyo, Japan

Date of Death
September 29, 2007

Nationality
Japanese

EDUCATION

Bachelor of Science (Chemistry)
Toho University
1943

Doctor of Philosophy (Chemistry)
University of Tokyo
1957

CAREER

1953-1957	Researcher, Meteorological Research Institute, Japan
1957-1958	Researcher, Scripps Institution of Oceanography, USA
1958-1967	Assistant Professor, Tokyo Woman's Christian University
1967-1974	Associate Professor, Tokyo Woman's Christian University
1974-1985	Professor, Tokyo Woman's Christian University
1981-1988	President, Geochemical Laboratory, Japan

NOTABLE CONTRIBUTIONS

- Pioneered research on radioactive fallout and its distribution in seawater, becoming a leading authority in marine geochemistry.
- Developed the "Saruhashi Table," a tool that measures the concentration of carbonic acid in seawater, helping to assess ocean acidification.
- Conducted extensive research on the carbon dioxide content in the atmosphere and its effects on marine ecosystems.
- Advocated for the peaceful use of nuclear energy and campaigned against nuclear weapons testing.
- Promoted opportunities for women in science and established the Saruhashi Prize to recognize female researchers' achievements.

ROSALIND FRANKLIN

CHEMIST AND X-RAY CRYSTALLOGRAPHER

PROFILE

Full Name
Rosalind Elsie Franklin

Date of Birth
July 25, 1920

Place of Birth
Notting Hill, London, England

Date of Death
April 16, 1958

Nationality
British

EDUCATION

- 1938: Enrolled at Newnham College, University of Cambridge, to study natural sciences.

- 1941: Graduated with second-class honors in chemistry.

CAREER

1947 Joined the Laboratoire Central des Services Chimiques de l'Etat in Paris, working on X-ray crystallography.

1951 Moved to King's College London to work under John Randall, focusing on DNA and RNA structure.

CONTRIBUTIONS AND ACHIEVEMENTS

- Pioneered X-ray crystallography techniques to study the structure of DNA, RNA, and viruses.
- Captured crucial X-ray diffraction images of DNA, including Photo 51, which provided evidence for the double-helix structure.
- Her work significantly contributed to the discovery of the DNA double helix by James Watson and Francis Crick.

LEGACY AND IMPACT

- Rosalind Franklin's groundbreaking research in X-ray crystallography played a crucial role in the understanding of DNA's structure.
- Despite her untimely death, her work posthumously received recognition for its fundamental contribution to the field of molecular biology.

Rosalyn Yalow

Nuclear Physicist

EDUCATION

1941 Graduated magna cum laude with a bachelor's degree in physics from Hunter College.

1945 Earned a Ph.D. in physics from the University of Illinois at Urbana-Champaign.

LEGACY AND IMPACT

- Rosalyn Yalow's groundbreaking research in RIA profoundly impacted medical diagnostics and facilitated advancements in endocrinology.

- Her work significantly improved the understanding and management of various diseases, particularly diabetes.

PROFILE

- **Full Name:** Rosalyn Sussman Yalow

- **Date of Birth:** July 19, 1921

- **Place of Birth:** Bronx, New York City, USA

- **Date of Death:** May 30, 2011

- **Nationality:** America

CAREER

1946 Joined the Veterans Administration Hospital in the Bronx as a staff physicist.

1950 Began her collaboration with Solomon Berson, leading to pioneering research in radioimmunoassays.

CONTRIBUTIONS AND ACHIEVEMENTS

- Pioneered the development and application of radioimmunoassay (RIA) techniques to measure hormones and other substances in the blood.

- Co-discovered the radioimmunoassay for insulin, a breakthrough that revolutionized the diagnosis and treatment of diabetes.

- Awarded the Nobel Prize in Physiology or Medicine in 1977 for her significant contributions to the field of endocrinology.

MARY JACKSON

Mathematician and Aerospace Engineer

PROFILE

Full Name

Mary Winston Jackson

Date of Birth

April 9, 1921

Place of Birth

Hampton, Virginia, USA

Date of Death

February 11, 2005

Nationality

American

EDUCATION

1942: Graduated with honors from Hampton Institute (now Hampton University) with a dual degree in mathematics and physical science.

CAREER

1951 Joined the National Advisory Committee for Aeronautics (NACA), which later became NASA.

1958 Transitioned from a human computer to an engineer at NASA, focusing on aerospace engineering.

CONTRIBUTIONS AND ACHIEVEMENTS

- Pioneered as one of the first African-American female engineers at NASA, breaking barriers of gender and racial discrimination.

- Played a significant role in the development of wind tunnel experiments and data analysis for NASA's aircraft and spacecraft.

- Conducted critical research on airflow and aerodynamics, contributing to the success of various space missions.

MARIE VAN BRITTAN BROWN

NURSE AND INNOVATOR

CAREER

1966   Co-invented the first home security system with her husband, Albert Brown, amid rising crime rates in their neighborhood.

1969   Received a patent for the home security system.

CONTRIBUTIONS

- Pioneered the concept of the home security system, which included a closed-circuit television (CCTV) system, a two-way communication device, and a remote-controlled door locking mechanism.
- Her invention revolutionized home security, laying the groundwork for modern security systems used worldwide.
- Marie Van Brittan Brown's invention was particularly significant for enhancing safety and security in urban environments.

LEGACY AND IMPACT

- Marie Van Brittan Brown's innovative home security system patent remains a groundbreaking contribution to the field of security and surveillance.
- Her work has influenced the development of advanced security systems used in homes, businesses, and public spaces.

PROFILE

Date of Birth
October 30, 1922

Place of Birth
Jamaica, Queens, New York City, USA

Date of Death
February 2, 1999

Nationality
American

EDUCATION

- Attended a nursing school to become a licensed nurse.

RAJESHWARI CHATTERJEE

SCIENTIST

PROFILE

Date of Birth: January 24, 1922

Place of Birth: Bangalore, India

Date of Death: September 3, 2010

Nationality: Indian

EDUCATION

1943 Bachelor of Science (B.Sc.) in Physics from Central College, Bangalore, India

1945 Master of Science (M.Sc.) in Physics from Central College, Bangalore, India

1951 Doctorate (D.Sc.) in Microwave Electronics from the University of London, UK

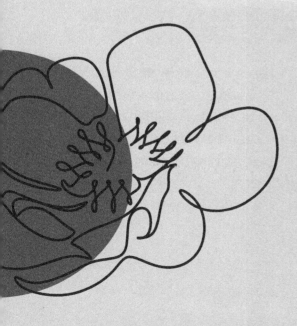

CAREER AND CONTRIBUTIONS

- Rajeshwari Chatterjee was an Indian physicist and renowned microwave engineer.
- She made significant contributions to the field of microwave engineering and semiconductor devices.
- In 1951, she became the first woman engineer from Karnataka, India.
- She joined the Indian Institute of Science (IISc), Bangalore, as a faculty member in 1952.
- Chatterjee's research on microwave engineering led to advancements in radar technology and wireless communication.
- She played a vital role in the development of microwave engineering education and research in India.
- Chatterjee received several awards and honors during her career, recognizing her exceptional contributions to science and engineering.

Stephanie Kwolek

Chemist

Profile

Full Name
Stephanie Louise Kwolek

Date of Birth
July 31, 1923

Place of Birth
New Kensington,
Pennsylvania, USA

Date of Death
June 18, 2014

Nationality
American

Education

1946
Graduated with a bachelor's degree in chemistry from Margaret Morrison Carnegie College (now part of Carnegie Mellon University).

Career

1946 Joined DuPont's research and development team, where she spent her entire career.

1965 Invented Kevlar, a strong and lightweight synthetic fiber with remarkable tensile strength.

Contributions

- Pioneered the invention of Kevlar, a high-performance material used in bullet-resistant vests, helmets, and numerous industrial applications.
- Kevlar's exceptional strength, heat resistance, and low weight revolutionized various industries, including aerospace, defense, and automotive.

Legacy and Impact

- Stephanie Kwolek's invention of Kevlar has saved countless lives, protecting law enforcement officers and military personnel from bullets and other threats.
- Her pioneering work in materials science and polymer chemistry continues to have a transformative impact on various industries.

Teruko Ishizaka

Scientist and Immunologist

PROFILE

Date of Birth
September 28, 1926

Place of Birth
Tokyo, Japan

Date of Death
June 4, 2019

Nationality
Japanese

EDUCATION

1949   Bachelor of Science in Agriculture from Tokyo University

1951   Master of Science in Bacteriology from Tokyo University

1959   Doctorate in Medical Science from Tokyo Women's Medical University

CAREER

Department of Immunology, Tokyo Women's Medical University

1950-1959	Research Associate
1959-1965	Assistant Professor
1965-1970	Associate Professor
1970-1990	Professor

School of Allied Health Sciences, Tokyo Women's Medical University

1984-1986	Dean

Graduate School of Health Sciences, Tokyo Women's Medical University

1988-1990	Dean

Tokyo Women's Medical University

1988-1990	Professor Emeritus

CONTRIBUTION

- Pioneered research in immunology, specifically the study of allergies and immune responses in the human body.
- Discovered the antibody class Immunoglobulin E (IgE), which plays a crucial role in allergic reactions.
- Her work helped in understanding the mechanisms behind allergic diseases and paved the way for advancements in allergy diagnosis and treatment.

VERA RUBIN
Astronomer

PROFILE

- **Full Name:** Vera Florence Cooper Rubin
- **Date of Birth:** July 23, 1928
- **Place of Birth:** Philadelphia, Pennsylvania, USA
- **Date of Death:** December 25, 2016
- **Nationality:** American

EDUCATION

- **1948** Graduated from Vassar College with a bachelor's degree in astronomy.
- **1954** Earned a master's degree in astronomy from Cornell University.

CAREER

- **1965** Joined the Carnegie Institution of Washington's Department of Terrestrial Magnetism.
- **1974** Discovered evidence for the existence of dark matter in galaxies, revolutionizing the understanding of the universe.

CONTRIBUTIONS

- Pioneered groundbreaking research in galaxy rotation curves, revealing the discrepancy between the observed motion of galaxies and the visible mass within them.
- Provided compelling evidence for the existence of dark matter, a mysterious form of matter that does not emit light and is thought to make up a significant portion of the universe's mass.
- Her work fundamentally changed the field of astronomy and cosmology, prompting further investigations into dark matter and its role in the universe's structure and evolution.

LEGACY AND IMPACT

- Vera Rubin's research on dark matter remains one of the most significant contributions to modern astrophysics.

Gloria Lim

Mycologist and Educator

Personal Information

Date of Birth: 1930   **Place of Birth:** Singapore

Date of Death: July 11, 2022   **Nationality:** Singaporean

Education

- Graduated with a BS in botany with first-class honors from the University of Singapore in 1954
- Earned a Diploma in Education in 1956 and an MS in plant pathology in 1957 from the University of Malaya in Kuala Lumpur
- Pursued further studies in mycology at the University of London and the University of California, Berkeley

Scientific and Academic Career

- Became an expert in mycology, focusing on tropical fungi and building up a repository of regional fungal species
- Served as Dean of the Faculty of Science at the University of Singapore in 1973 and again from 1979 to 1980, becoming the first woman to hold that position
- Played a key role in the development of the Department of Botany at the National University of Singapore (NUS)
- Appointed as the inaugural Director of the National Institute of Education (NIE) in 1991, where she helped establish fully accredited university-standard programs in education
- Served on the Public Service Commission (PSC) as its first woman commissioner for 14 years
- Acted as the General Manager of the Community Mediation Unit (CMU) for 8 years

Legacy and Impact

- Received the Bintang Bakti Masyarakat (Public Service Star) in 1993 for her contributions to the PSC
- Awarded an honorary Doctorate of Science from Loughborough University in England in 1999 for her contributions to science and education in Singapore
- Honored with the Distinguished Science Alumni Award from NUS in 2005
- Elected as a Fellow of the Singapore National Academy of Science in 2018

TU YOUYOU

PHARMACEUTICAL
CHEMIST AND
MALARIOLOGIST

PERSONAL INFORMATION

Full Name
Tu Youyou (屠呦呦)

Date of Birth
December 30, 1930

Place of Birth
Ningbo, Zhejiang, China

Nationality
Chinese

EDUCATION

1951 Graduated from Peking University Medical School (now Peking University Health Science Center).

CAREER

1969 Led a team of researchers during the Vietnam War to search for a treatment for malaria.

1972 Discovered the antimalarial compound artemisinin from the plant Artemisia annua, commonly known as sweet wormwood.

CONTRIBUTIONS AND ACHIEVEMENTS

- Pioneered the discovery and development of artemisinin, a highly effective and life-saving antimalarial drug.
- Artemisinin and its derivatives revolutionized malaria treatment, saving millions of lives and becoming a cornerstone of malaria control programs worldwide.
- Awarded the 2015 Nobel Prize in Physiology or Medicine for her significant contributions to global health and the fight against malaria.

LEGACY AND IMPACT

- Tu Youyou's groundbreaking discovery of artemisinin has had an immeasurable impact on global health, particularly in the battle against malaria.
- Her dedication and perseverance in finding a cure for malaria have inspired researchers and medical professionals worldwide to continue the fight against infectious diseases.
- Tu Youyou's Nobel Prize recognition elevated the importance of traditional Chinese medicine and natural product research in modern medicine.

Gelia Castillo

Sociologist

Profile

Date of Birth

December 25, 1933

Place of Birth

Manila, Philippines

Date of Death

March 5, 2017

Nationality

Filipino

Education

1954

Bachelor of Science in Food Technology from the University of the Philippines

1960

Master of Science in Rural Sociology from Pennsylvania State University

1965

Doctor of Philosophy in Sociology from Cornell University

Career

1954-1955 Research Assistant at the University of the Philippines' College of Agriculture

1961-1963 Research Associate at the International Rice Research Institute (IRRI)

1965-1966 Research Consultant at the United Nations Economic and Social Commission for Asia and the Pacific (UNESCAP)

1966-1972 Professor and Chair of the Department of Rural Sociology at the University of the Philippines Los Baños (UPLB)

1973-1984 Principal Scientist and Head of the Social Sciences Division at IRRI

1985-1989 Director of the Southeast Asian Regional Center for Graduate Study and Research in Agriculture (SEARCA)

Contributions

- Pioneered the field of rural sociology in the Philippines and Southeast Asia
- Championed gender-responsive and community-based research, focusing on the role of women in rural development
- Conducted extensive research on rural poverty, migration, and social change, influencing policies and programs in agricultural development and rural communities
- Played a key role in promoting women's empowerment and gender equality in the agricultural sector

PROFILE

Full Name

Patsy O'Connell Sherman

Date of Birth

December 15, 1930

Place of Birth

Minneapolis, Minnesota, USA

Date of Death

February 11, 2008

Nationality

American

EDUCATION

1952: Graduated from Gustavus Adolphus College with a bachelor's degree in chemistry.

PATSY SHERMAN

CHEMIST

CAREER

1952   Joined 3M (Minnesota Mining and Manufacturing Company) as a chemist in the research laboratory.

1956   Co-invented Scotchgard™, a stain and water repellent, with her colleague Samuel Smith.

CONTRIBUTIONS AND ACHIEVEMENTS

- Pioneered the invention of Scotchgard™, which revolutionized fabric protection and stain resistance.
- Scotchgard™ became widely used in various industries, from textiles and apparel to furniture and carpets, providing long-lasting protection against stains and spills.
- Patsy Sherman's work on Scotchgard™ received multiple patents and garnered significant commercial success for 3M.

LEGACY AND IMPACT

- Patsy Sherman's invention of Scotchgard™ had a transformative impact on everyday products, making them more durable and easier to maintain.

RUZENA BAJCSY

Engineer and Computer Scientist

PROFILE

Date of Birth
January 21, 1933

Place of Birth Bratislava, Czechoslovakia (now Slovakia)

Nationality
American

EDUCATION

1957: Earned a master's degree in electrical engineering from the Slovak University of Technology in Bratislava.

1963: Received a Ph.D. in electrical engineering from Stanford University.

CAREER

1969 Joined the Artificial Intelligence Laboratory at Stanford University as a research associate.

1972 Became a professor at the University of Pennsylvania and founded the General Robotics and Active Sensory Perception (GRASP) Laboratory.

CONTRIBUTIONS AND ACHIEVEMENTS

- Pioneered research in robotics, computer vision, and artificial intelligence, making significant contributions to the field.
- Developed pioneering techniques for computer vision, such as active contour models (snakes), which are widely used in image processing and object recognition.
- Advocated for interdisciplinary research, bridging computer science, robotics, and biology, leading to innovative approaches in medical imaging and healthcare technology.

Jane Goodall

CAREER

1960 Began her groundbreaking research on wild chimpanzees at the Gombe Stream National Park in Tanzania.

1965 Published her first scientific paper, becoming the first person to observe chimpanzees making and using tools.

1977 Founded the Jane Goodall Institute (JGI) to support wildlife conservation and community development.

CONTRIBUTIONS

- Pioneered groundbreaking research on chimpanzee behavior, challenging prevailing notions of human uniqueness and intelligence.

- Made significant discoveries, such as chimpanzees using tools for various purposes and exhibiting complex social behaviors.

- Dedicated her life to wildlife conservation and environmental advocacy, raising awareness about endangered species and habitat protection.

PROFILE

Full Name
Jane Goodall, DBE

Date of Birth
April 3, 1934

Place of Birth
London, England

Nationality
British

EDUCATION

1966: Earned a Ph.D. in ethology from the University of Cambridge, studying the behavior of wild chimpanzees in Tanzania.

MARGARET HAMILTON

COMPUTER SCIENTIST, SYSTEMS ENGINEER, AND BUSINESS OWNER

PROFILE

Full Name
Margaret Heafield Hamilton

Date of Birth
August 17, 1936

Place of Birth
Paoli, Indiana, USA

Nationality
American

EDUCATION

1958
Graduated with a bachelor's degree in mathematics from Earlham College.

1960
Earned a master's degree in mathematics from the University of Michigan.

CAREER

1961 Joined MIT's Instrumentation Laboratory (now Draper) as a programmer for the Semi-Automatic Ground Environment (SAGE) project.

1969 Led the software team for the Apollo space program at MIT, overseeing the development of the on-board flight software for the Apollo guidance computer.

Contributions

- Pioneered the development of software and systems engineering concepts for real-time, mission-critical applications.
- Led the design and implementation of the on-board flight software for the Apollo missions, including Apollo 11, the first manned moon landing.
- Introduced the concept of asynchronous software, which allowed priority scheduling and error detection in space missions.

Legacy and Impact

- Developed the concept of error detection and recovery, which was crucial during the Apollo 11 mission when the guidance computer was overloaded.

ADA
YONATH
CHEMIST AND CRYSTALLOGRAPHER

PROFILE

Full Name
Ada E. Yonath

Date of Birth
June 22, 1939

Place of Birth
Jerusalem, British Mandate of Palestine (now Israel)

Nationality
Israeli

EDUCATION

1962
Bachelor's Degree in Chemistry, The Hebrew University of Jerusalem

1968
Ph.D. in X-ray Crystallography, Weizmann Institute of Science

CAREER

1970   Joined the Weizmann Institute of Science as a Staff Scientist, specializing in X-ray crystallography.

Pioneered research in X-ray crystallography, with a focus on ribosomes, the cellular structures responsible for protein synthesis.

Developed innovative methods for studying ribosomal structures at the atomic level, contributing to the understanding of the ribosome's function.

1979   Became the Head of the Max-Planck-Research Unit for Ribosomal Structure in Hamburg, Germany.

Determined the first high-resolution structure of the ribosome, providing crucial insights into its complex mechanism.

Her work shed light on the process of protein synthesis, laying the groundwork for understanding antibiotic resistance and drug development.

2009   Awarded the Nobel Prize in Chemistry for her groundbreaking work on the structure and function of the ribosome.

ANGELITA CASTRO KELLY

Space Scientist and Physicist

PROFILE

Full Name

Angelita Albano Castro Kelly

Date of Birth

August 26, 1942

Place of Birth

Jones, Isabela, Philippines

Date of Death

June 7, 2015

Nationality

Filipino-American

EDUCATION

Bachelor's degree in Mathematics and Physics

University of Santo Tomas

1962

Master's degree in Physics

University of Maryland

CAREER

- Space scientist and physicist with 12 years of service at NASA
- Started as a data analyst for the Goddard Space Flight Center Spacelab Data Processing Facility (SLDPF) in 1977
- First female Mission Operations Manager (MOM) of NASA's Earth Observing System (EOS) project in 1990
- Spearheaded and supervised the developmental stage of the three EOS missions: Terra, Aqua, and Aura
- Developed overall mission operations concepts, ensuring the implementation of mission requirements
- Served a dual role as the Earth Science Constellation Manager during her time at NASA

LEGACY

- Pioneering figure as the first female MOM of NASA
- Spearheaded critical missions in the Earth Observing System, contributing to the understanding of land, water, and atmosphere phenomena
- Recognized for her expertise and contributions with numerous accolades from the Philippines government and NASA
- Listed as one of the 100 Most Influential Filipina Women in the United States by the Filipina Women's Network

CHRISTIANE NÜSSLEIN-VOLHARD

Developmental Biologist

PROFILE

Date of Birth
October 20, 1942

Place of Birth
Magdeburg, Germany

Nationality
German

EDUCATION

1962
Bachelor's Degree in Biology, Johann Wolfgang Goethe University Frankfurt

1968
Ph.D. in Genetics, University of Tübingen

CAREER

1978 - Present
- Director, Max Planck Institute for Developmental Biology, Tübingen, Germany.
- Pioneered groundbreaking research in developmental biology, particularly in understanding the genetic mechanisms of early embryonic development in fruit flies (Drosophila melanogaster).
- Co-discovered the homeobox genes and their role in regulating the formation of body segments and organs during embryonic development.
- Conducted extensive studies on the genetic control of pattern formation, providing insights into the fundamental processes that shape the animal body plan.

1995
- Awarded the Nobel Prize in Physiology or Medicine, along with Eric Wieschaus and Edward B. Lewis, for their discoveries concerning the genetic control of early embryonic development.

CONTRIBUTIONS

- Christiane Nüsslein-Volhard's research has significantly advanced the field of developmental biology, providing fundamental insights into the genetic basis of embryonic development.

JOCELYN BELL BURNELL

ASTROPHYSICIST

PROFILE

Date of Birth: July 15, 1943

Place of Birth: Lurgan, Northern Ireland

Nationality: British

EDUCATION

1965 Graduated with a bachelor's degree in physics from the University of Glasgow.

1969 Earned a Ph.D. in radio astronomy from the University of Cambridge.

CONTRIBUTIONS

- Co-discovered pulsars, rapidly rotating neutron stars that emit beams of electromagnetic radiation, a groundbreaking discovery in radio astronomy.

- Her discovery of pulsars opened up new avenues of research, leading to significant advancements in our understanding of neutron stars and compact objects.

CAREER

1967 - 1973 Conducted groundbreaking research as a graduate student at the University of Cambridge, leading to the discovery of pulsars.

1974 - 1977 Research Fellow at the University of Southampton, investigating X-ray sources in the universe.

1978 - 1982 Staff astronomer at the Royal Observatory, Edinburgh, contributing to various radio astronomy projects.

1982 - PRESENT Professor of Astrophysics, University of Oxford, conducting research and mentoring students.

LEGACY AND IMPACT

- Despite being overlooked for the Nobel Prize in Physics for the discovery, Burnell's contribution has been widely recognized, and she has become a prominent role model for women in science.

Antonia Novello

Former United States Surgeon General

Personal Information

Full Name: Antonia Coello Novello

Date of Birth: August 23, 1944

Place of Birth: Fajardo, Puerto Rico

Nationality: American

Education

1965 Graduated with a bachelor's degree in biology from the University of Puerto Rico.

1970 Earned a medical degree (M.D.) from the University of Puerto Rico School of Medicine.

Career

1973 - 1976 Internship and Residency in Pediatrics at the University of Michigan Medical Center.

1976 - 1985 Served as Director of Ambulatory Pediatric Clinic and later Chief of the Division of Pediatric Nephrology at the University of Michigan Medical Center.

1985 - 1986 Visiting Scientist and Research Fellow at the National Institute of Arthritis, Metabolism, and Digestive Diseases (NIAMDD).

1986 - 1990 Deputy Director of the National Institute of Child Health and Human Development (NICHD).

1990 - 1993 Appointed as the 14th United States Surgeon General, the first woman and first Hispanic to hold the position.

1993 - Present Distinguished Professor of Health Policy at the George Mason University Schar School of Policy and Government.

Contributions and Achievements

- Made significant contributions to the field of pediatric nephrology, particularly in research related to kidney disease in children.
- As Surgeon General, led public health campaigns focused on smoking cessation, AIDS awareness, and health disparities.

OLGA D. GONZÁLEZ-SANABRIA

Scientist and Inventor

PROFILE

○ **Place of Birth:** Puerto Rico

EDUCATION

○ Master of Science in Chemical Engineering, University of Toledo, Ohio

○ Bachelor of Science in Chemical Engineering, University of Puerto Rico at Mayaguez

CAREER

NASA Glenn Research Center

- Director of Engineering and Technical Services, overseeing a range of integrated services, including engineering, fabrication, testing, facility management, and aircraft services.
- Played an instrumental role in the development of "Long Cycle-Life Nickel-Hydrogen Batteries," contributing to the power system of the International Space Station.
- Held the position of Director of the Systems Management Office, implementing Glenn's Business Management System, earning ISO 9000 certification.

ACHIEVEMENTS

- Recognized as the highest-ranking Hispanic at NASA Glenn Research Center.
- Awarded the NASA Outstanding Leadership Medal for exceptional contributions to the organization.
- Received the NASA Exceptional Service Medal for outstanding service and dedication to NASA's mission.
- Honored with the Women of Color in Technology Career Achievement Award for breaking barriers in the field of engineering.
- Inducted into the Ohio Women's Hall of Fame as a distinguished scientist, inventor, and executive.

MARY-CLAIRE KING

GENETICIST

CAREER AND CONTRIBUTIONS

- Identified the first breast cancer gene, BRCA1, through her pioneering research on genetic linkage analysis. Her discovery revolutionized our understanding of inherited breast cancer and laid the foundation for genetic testing and personalized medicine.

- Advocated for the use of DNA sequencing technology in solving human rights issues, including identifying victims of human rights abuses and reuniting families separated by conflicts or disasters.

- Played a critical role in identifying "The Disappeared" of Argentina during the military dictatorship and in identifying victims of the Chilean dictatorship.

- Her work on the genetic relatedness of human populations has shed light on human evolution, migration patterns, and genetic diversity.

- Served as a professor at the University of California, Berkeley, and the University of Washington, where she mentored numerous students and researchers in the field of genetics.

PROFILE

Date of Birth
February 27, 1946

Place of Birth
Evanston, Illinois, USA

Date of Death
April 16, 1958

Nationality
American

EDUCATION

Bachelor's degree in Mathematics
Carleton College
1967

Ph.D. in Genetics
University of California, Berkeley
1973

FRANÇOISE BARRÉ-SINOUSSI

VIROLOGIST

ABOUT ME

Date of Birth
July 30, 1947

Place of Birth
Paris, France

Nationality
French

EDUCATION

1966 Earned undergraduate degree in Natural Sciences from the University of Paris

1974 obtained her doctorate in Science at the Pasteur Institute

CAREER

- Dr. Barré-Sinoussi joined the Pasteur Institute in Paris in 1971, and this is where she would make her most significant contributions to science.

- Alongside her mentor and collaborator, Luc Montagnier, she co-discovered the human immunodeficiency virus (HIV) in 1983. Their research identified and characterized the virus as the cause of AIDS, a critical milestone in the fight against the disease.

- The discovery of HIV and its association with AIDS led to a deeper understanding of the virus's transmission and pathogenesis. This breakthrough opened doors for the development of antiretroviral therapies that have saved countless lives and transformed the course of the AIDS epidemic.

TEMPLE GRANDIN

Academic and Animal Behaviorist

Full Name: Mary Temple Grandin

Date of Birth: August 29, 1947

Place of Birth: Boston, Massachusetts, USA

Nationality: American

EDUCATION

Bachelor of Psychology
Franklin Pierce College, USA (1970)

Master of Animal Science
Arizona State University, USA (1975)

Doctor of Animal Science
University of Illinois at Urbana-Champaign, USA (1989)

CAREER

- Professor of Animal Science at Colorado State University.
- Renowned animal behaviorist, advocate for animal welfare, and consultant to the livestock industry.
- Diagnosed with autism at an early age and became an advocate for individuals with autism spectrum disorders.

NOTABLE ACHIEVEMENTS

- Pioneered humane livestock handling techniques, designing livestock handling facilities that minimize stress and improve animal welfare.
- Developed the "hug box" (squeeze machine) to help calm and comfort individuals with autism, inspired by her own experiences.
- Authored several books on autism, animal behavior, and her life experiences, including "Thinking in Pictures" and "The Autistic Brain."

PROFILE

Full Name

Yee-Ching Wong-Staal (known as Flossie Wong-Staal)

Date of Birth

August 27, 1946

Place of Birth

Guangzhou, China

Nationality

American

EDUCATION

- **1964:** Graduated with a bachelor's degree in Bacteriology from the University of California, Los Angeles (UCLA).
- **1972:** Earned a Ph.D. in Molecular Biology from the University of California, Los Angeles (UCLA).

FLOSSIE WONG-STAAL

VIROLOGIST AND MOLECULAR BIOLOGIST

CAREER

1973 - 1985	Research Scientist at the National Cancer Institute (NCI), where she contributed to the discovery of reverse transcriptase in retroviruses.
1986 - 1990	Professor at the University of California, San Diego (UCSD), and the first scientist to clone and characterize HIV.
1990 - 2002	Director of the Institute for Human Virology and Chief of the Division of Virology at the University of Maryland School of Medicine.
2002 - 2010	Chief Scientific Officer at Immusol, Inc., a biotechnology company focusing on gene-based therapies.
2010 - 2015	Served as a Presidential Chair Professor at the University of California, Riverside (UCR), and the Director of the Center for AIDS Research and Education.

CONTRIBUTIONS AND ACHIEVEMENTS

- Pioneered research on retroviruses, including HIV, leading to significant advancements in the understanding of viral replication and infection mechanisms.

- Co-discovered HIV as the cause of AIDS and played a crucial role in the development of diagnostic tests for HIV infection.

- Made significant contributions to the development of gene-based therapies and the use of RNA interference for treating viral infections and other diseases.

LINDA BROWN BUCK

BIOLOGIST

PROFILE

Date of Birth
January 29, 1947

Place of Birth
Seattle, Washington, USA

Nationality
American

EDUCATION

Ph.D. in Immunology
University of Texas
Southwestern Medical
Center at Dallas

B.S. in Psychology and Microbiology
University of Washington,
Seattle

CAREER

- Assistant Professor, Neurobiology Department, Harvard Medical School
- Investigator, Howard Hughes Medical Institute
- Member, Division of Basic Sciences, Fred Hutchinson Cancer Research Center
- Affiliate Professor of Physiology and Biophysics, University of Washington, Seattle

RESEARCH AND ACCOMPLISHMENTS

- Awarded the Nobel Prize in Physiology or Medicine in 2004, along with Richard Axel, for the discovery of odorant receptors and the organization of the olfactory system.
- Pioneered the identification of odorant receptors and demonstrated the existence of a large and diverse multigene family responsible for detecting thousands of different odorous chemicals.
- Uncovered the organization of odorant receptors in the olfactory epithelium and olfactory bulb, revealing a highly distributed and combinatorial system for encoding odors.
- Investigated the mechanisms underlying odor perception and the integration of olfactory information in the olfactory cortex.
- Explored the neural circuits involved in innate behaviors, including the detection of pheromones and basic drives such as fear, appetite, and reproduction.
- Developed high-throughput molecular techniques to study aging and lifespan, searching for central mechanisms that regulate aging and cell aging throughout the body.

ELIZABETH BLACKBURN

BIOLOGIST

Date of Birth: November 26, 1948
Place of Birth: Hobart, Tasmania, Australia
Nationality: Australian-American

EDUCATION

1970 — Bachelor of Science in Biochemistry and Microbiology, University of Melbourne, Australia

1975 — Ph.D. in Molecular Biology, University of Cambridge, United Kingdom

CAREER

1987-1990 — Professor of Microbiology and Immunology, University of California, Berkeley

1990-1993 — Professor of Microbiology and Immunology, UCSF

1993-2016 — Professor of Microbiology and Immunology, UCSF, and Morris Herzstein Endowed Chair in Biology and Physiology

2016-2020 — President of the Salk Institute for Biological Studies, La Jolla, California

2017-present — Professor Emerita, UCSF

RESEARCH AND ACCOMPLISHMENTS

- Elizabeth Blackburn, along with Carol W. Greider and Jack W. Szostak, discovered telomerase, an enzyme that maintains the length of telomeres, the protective caps at the ends of chromosomes. This groundbreaking work earned them the Nobel Prize in Physiology or Medicine in 2009.
- Her research on telomeres and telomerase has contributed to our understanding of cellular aging and has implications for age-related diseases, including cancer.
- She has made significant contributions to elucidating the roles of telomeres in cellular division, genetic stability, and cellular senescence.
- Blackburn's work has shed light on the interplay between telomeres, cellular health, and stress, providing new insights into the impact of lifestyle and environmental factors on aging.
- In addition to the Nobel Prize, she has received numerous other awards and honors, including the Lasker Award, Canada Gairdner International Award, and the Breakthrough Prize in Life Sciences.

MAZLAN BINTI OTHMAN

Astrophysicist

PROFILE

Date of Birth
1951

Place of Birth
Malaysia

Nationality
Malaysian

EDUCATION

Dr. Mazlan Othman obtained her education in Malaysia and pursued her interest in astrophysics.

She earned her Ph.D. in Physics and specialized in the study of cosmic rays, high-energy astrophysics, and space science.

CONTRIBUTIONS AND IMPACT

- Dr. Othman has made significant contributions to the field of space science and astrophysics, with a focus on understanding cosmic rays and high-energy phenomena in the universe.
- She served as the founding director of the Malaysian National Space Agency (ANGKASA) and played a crucial role in advancing Malaysia's space science and technology capabilities.
- Dr. Othman is known for her dedication to promoting science and education, particularly in the areas of space exploration and astronomy, both in Malaysia and internationally.

SCIENCE DIPLOMACY

- One of Dr. Othman's notable achievements is her role as the first Director of the United Nations Office for Outer Space Affairs (UNOOSA).
- As the head of UNOOSA, she was instrumental in promoting international cooperation in the peaceful uses of outer space and enhancing global collaboration in space-related activities.

Adriana Ocampo

PLANETARY GEOLOGIST AND A SCIENCE PROGRAM MANAGER

- **Full Name:** Adriana C. Ocampo
- **Nationality:** Colombian
- **Date of Birth:** 1955

EDUCATION

- Bachelor's Degree in Geology, Universidad de Los Andes, Colombia
- Master's Degree in Science, California State University, Northridge
- Doctorate Degree in Geology, University of London, Imperial College

CAREER

- Planetary Geologist and Science Program Manager at NASA Jet Propulsion Laboratory (JPL).
- Participated in various NASA space missions, including the Galileo mission to Jupiter and the New Horizons mission to Pluto.
- Served as the Science Program Manager for the Juno mission to Jupiter and the Psyche mission to explore a metal asteroid.

NOTABLE ACHIEVEMENTS

- Recognized for her expertise in planetary geology and her significant contributions to the study of celestial bodies in our solar system.
- Led scientific teams in analyzing data and discoveries from space missions, advancing our understanding of the geology and history of other planets.

LEGACY AND IMPACT

- Adriana Ocampo's pioneering research in planetary geology and her involvement in various space missions have significantly advanced our knowledge of other planets and celestial bodies.

Susan Solomon
Atmospheric Chemist

Career

- After her doctoral studies, Solomon worked as a research scientist at the National Oceanic and Atmospheric Administration (NOAA) in Boulder, Colorado.
- In 1988, she joined the National Center for Atmospheric Research (NCAR) in Boulder as a senior scientist, becoming a prominent figure in atmospheric chemistry.
- Throughout her career, she held various academic and research positions at leading institutions, including MIT (Massachusetts Institute of Technology) and the University of Colorado Boulder.

Profile

Date of Birth   January 19, 1956

Place of Birth   Illinois, USA

Nationality   American

Contributions

- Solomon is renowned for her pivotal role in identifying the causes of the Antarctic ozone hole, one of the most significant discoveries in atmospheric science.
- Her research led to the understanding of the role of human-made chlorofluorocarbons (CFCs) in ozone depletion, emphasizing the importance of international actions to address this environmental issue.
- Her work was instrumental in the negotiation and adoption of the Montreal Protocol in 1987, an international treaty aimed at phasing out ozone-depleting substances, which has successfully protected the ozone layer.

Education

Bachelor of Arts degree in Chemistry
Illinois Institute of Technology
1977

Ph.D. in Chemistry
University of California, Berkeley
1981

Frances Arnold

Chemical Engineer

CAREER AND ACCOMPLISHMENTS

- Frances Arnold is the Linus Pauling Professor of Chemical Engineering, Bioengineering, and Biochemistry at the California Institute of Technology (Caltech).
- She is a pioneer in the field of directed evolution, which involves harnessing the power of evolution to create new enzymes or optimize existing ones for various applications, including industrial processes and pharmaceuticals.
- Arnold's groundbreaking work in directed evolution has significant implications for green chemistry, renewable energy, and sustainable processes, as it allows for the creation of more efficient and environmentally friendly chemical reactions.
- In recognition of her outstanding contributions to the field, Frances Arnold was awarded the Nobel Prize in Chemistry in 2018, becoming the fifth woman in history to receive this prestigious award in chemistry.

EDUCATION

1979 Bachelor of Science in Mechanical and Aerospace Engineering, Princeton University

1981 Master of Science in Chemical Engineering, University of California, Berkeley

1985 Ph.D. in Chemical Engineering, University of California, Berkele

PROFILE

- **Full Name:** Frances Hamilton Arnold

- **Date of Birth:** July 25, 1956

- **Place of Birth:** Pennsylvania, U.S.A

- **Nationality:** America

Donna Strickland

PHYSICIST

PROFILE

Full Name
Donna Theo Strickland

Date of Birth
May 27, 1959

Place of Birth
Guelph, Ontario, Canada

Nationality
Canadian

EDUCATION

Bachelor of Engineering Physics
McMaster University, Canada, 1981

Doctor of Philosophy (Ph.D.) in Optics
University of Rochester, USA, 1989

CAREER

National Research Council Canada

1981-1985 Associate Research Officer

Department of Physics and Astronomy, University of Waterloo, Canada

1988-1992 Assistant Professor

1992-1997 Associate Professor

1997-present Full Professor

NOTABLE ACHIEVEMENTS

- Co-developed chirped pulse amplification (CPA) technique for generating high-intensity, ultra-short laser pulses, which revolutionized laser physics and earned the 2018 Nobel Prize in Physics.

- Her groundbreaking work with CPA opened up new avenues for research in various fields, including medical imaging and precision manufacturing.

- Recognized for her contributions to the field of optics and lasers, inspiring many young scientists, particularly women, to pursue careers in science and technology.

CAROLYN WIDNEY GREIDER

MOLECULAR BIOLOGIST

PROFILE

Date of Birth: April 15, 1961

Place of Birth: San Diego, California, U.S.A

Nationality: American

EDUCATION

1983 Bachelor of Science in Biology, University of California, Santa Barbara

1987 Ph.D. in Molecular Biology, University of California, Berkeley

CAREER AND ACCOMPLISHMENTS

- Carolyn Widney Greider is a molecular biologist and professor at Johns Hopkins University School of Medicine.
- She is best known for her groundbreaking research on telomeres and telomerase, which are crucial components of the cellular aging process and play a role in protecting the integrity of chromosomes.
- In 1984, as a graduate student at the University of California, Berkeley, Greider, along with her research advisor Elizabeth Blackburn and Jack Szostak, co-discovered telomerase, an enzyme that helps maintain the length and stability of telomeres.
- This discovery was of significant importance, as it provided fundamental insights into how cells protect their genetic information and contributed to our understanding of aging and cancer.
- In recognition of her pioneering work, Carolyn Widney Greider was awarded the Nobel Prize in Physiology or Medicine in 2009, sharing the honor with Elizabeth Blackburn and Jack Szostak.

KALPANA CHAWLA

ASTRONAUT AND AEROSPACE ENGINEER

Date of Birth: March 17, 1962
Place of Birth: Karnal, Haryana, India
Date of Death: February 1, 2003
Nationality: Indian-American

NOTABLE ACHIEVEMENTS

- Demonstrated exceptional skills as an astronaut and contributed to scientific research in microgravity and material sciences during her space missions.
- Played a vital role in conducting experiments and deploying satellites during her time aboard the Space Shuttle missions.

AWARDS AND HONORS

- Awarded the Congressional Space Medal of Honor, NASA Space Flight Medal, and NASA Distinguished Service Medal posthumously.

EDUCATION

- Bachelor of Engineering in Aeronautical Engineering, Punjab Engineering College, India
- Master of Science in Aerospace Engineering, University of Texas at Arlington, USA
- Doctorate in Aerospace Engineering, University of Colorado Boulder, USA

CAREER

- Aerospace engineer, research scientist, and NASA astronaut.
- Joined NASA in 1995 and became the first woman of Indian origin to fly in space.
- Served as a mission specialist on Space Shuttle Columbia STS-87 (1997) and STS-107 (2003) missions.

LEGACY AND IMPACT

- Kalpana Chawla's life and achievements have inspired millions worldwide, particularly women, to pursue careers in science, technology, engineering, and mathematics (STEM) fields.
- Her tragic loss during the Space Shuttle Columbia disaster serves as a reminder of the risks and challenges associated with space exploration, reinforcing the importance of safety and continuous improvement in space missions.

Jennifer Anne Doudna

Biochemist and Molecular Biologist

Personal Information

Date of Birth: February 19, 1964
Place of Birth: Washington, D.C., USA
Nationality: American

Education

1985 Bachelor of Arts in Biochemistry, Pomona College

1989 Ph.D. in Biological Chemistry and Molecular Pharmacology, Harvard University

Career and Accomplishments

- Jennifer Doudna is a professor of biochemistry, biophysics, and structural biology at the University of California, Berkeley.

- She is a pioneer in the field of CRISPR-Cas9 gene editing, a revolutionary tool that allows precise and efficient editing of DNA sequences in various organisms.

- Along with her collaborator Emmanuelle Charpentier, Jennifer Doudna demonstrated the programmable nature of CRISPR-Cas9, enabling it to be used as a highly versatile and powerful gene-editing tool.

- Their seminal work was published in 2012, and the CRISPR-Cas9 technology has since become widely adopted in laboratories worldwide for various applications in genetic research, biotechnology, and medicine.

- In recognition of their groundbreaking work, Jennifer Doudna and Emmanuelle Charpentier were awarded the Nobel Prize in Chemistry in 2020.

- Doudna has received numerous other awards and honors for her scientific contributions, including being elected to the National Academy of Sciences and the National Academy of Medicine.

Andrea Mia Ghez

Astrophysicist

Career

- Ghez joined the faculty at UCLA (University of California, Los Angeles) in 1994, where she currently holds the Lauren B. Leichtman & Arthur E. Levine Chair in Astrophysics.
- She is also the Director of the UCLA Galactic Center Group, which focuses on studying the center of our galaxy and its supermassive black hole.

Contributions

- One of Andrea Ghez's most significant contributions is her work on studying the motion of stars near the center of the Milky Way galaxy.
- Using high-resolution imaging techniques, Ghez and her team were able to observe the orbits of stars very close to the supermassive black hole located at the center of our galaxy, known as Sagittarius A*.
- Her research provided strong evidence for the existence of a supermassive black hole at the center of the Milky Way and offered valuable insights into the dynamics of stars in the vicinity of black holes.

Award

- In 2020, she was awarded the Nobel Prize in Physics, sharing it with Reinhard Genzel, for her discoveries related to the center of our galaxy and the existence of a supermassive black hole.
- Ghez has also received the Crafoord Prize in Astronomy (2020) and the Benjamin Franklin Medal in Physics (2021).

Profile

Date of Birth
June 16, 1965

Place of Birth
New York City, USA

Nationality
American

Education

Bachelor of Science in Physics
Massachusetts Institute of Technology (MIT)
1987

Ph.D. in Astronomy
California Institute of Technology (Caltech)
1992

CAROLYN RUTH BERTOZZI

Chemist

PROFILE

Date of Birth
November 10, 1966

Place of Birth
Boston, Massachusetts,
USA

Nationality
American

EDUCATION

1988
Bachelor of Science degree in
Chemistry
Harvard University

1993
Ph.D. in Chemistry
University of California,
Berkeley

CAREER

- After her doctoral studies, Bertozzi conducted postdoctoral research at the University of California, San Francisco.
- In 1996, she joined the faculty at the University of California, Berkeley, as an assistant professor in the Department of Chemistry.

CONTRIBUTIONS

- One of Carolyn Bertozzi's significant contributions is her development and advancement of bioorthogonal chemistry, a field that focuses on the chemical reactions that can occur inside living organisms without interfering with their natural biological processes.
- She has made significant contributions to the development of new chemical reactions and tools that allow researchers to label and modify biomolecules in living systems with precision and specificity.
- Bertozzi's work in bioorthogonal chemistry has found applications in various fields, including biotechnology, drug development, and the study of complex biological processes.

AWARDS

- In 2022, Carolyn Bertozzi was awarded the Nobel Prize in Chemistry, jointly with Morten P. Meldal and Karl Barry Sharpless, "for the development of click chemistry and bioorthogonal chemistry".

NERGIS MAVALVALA

Astrophysicist

CONTRIBUTIONS AND IMPACT

- Nergis Mavalvala is a leading expert in the field of gravitational-wave astronomy, a branch of astrophysics that studies the ripples in space-time caused by the most energetic events in the universe, such as black hole mergers and neutron star collisions.

- As a member of the Laser Interferometer Gravitational-Wave Observatory (LIGO) collaboration, she played a crucial role in the first direct detection of gravitational waves in 2015. This historic discovery confirmed a key prediction of Albert Einstein's theory of general relativity and opened a new era in astronomy.

- Her research involves the development and implementation of highly sensitive instruments and technologies to detect and study gravitational waves, contributing to advancements in gravitational-wave detection capabilities.

- Nergis Mavalvala has received numerous awards and honors for her contributions to science, including being elected as a fellow of the American Physical Society and the American Academy of Arts and Sciences.

PROFILE

Date of Birth: 1968
Place of Birth: Lahore, Pakistan
Nationality: Pakistani-American

EDUCATION

- Bachelor's degree in Physics and Astronomy, Wellesley College, Massachusetts, USA
- Ph.D. in Physics, Massachusetts Institute of Technology (MIT), Massachusetts, USA

EMMANUELLE MARIE CHARPENTIER

Microbiologist and Biochemist

EDUCATION

1992   **Master's degree in Biochemistry**
University Pierre-and-Marie-Curie, Paris, France

1995   **Ph.D. in Microbiology**
Institute Pasteur, Paris, France

PROFILE

Date of Birth: December 11, 1968

Place of Birth: Juvisy-sur-Orge, France

Nationality: French

CONTRIBUTIONS AND IMPACT

- Emmanuelle Charpentier is best known for her groundbreaking work in the field of gene editing using the CRISPR-Cas9 system. Along with her collaborator Jennifer Doudna, she developed the CRISPR-Cas9 gene editing technology, which has revolutionized the field of molecular biology and genetics.

- CRISPR-Cas9 allows precise and efficient editing of DNA, making it easier for researchers to modify genes in various organisms, including plants, animals, and even human cells. This technology has significant implications for medical research, agriculture, and potential gene therapies.

- For her groundbreaking work on CRISPR-Cas9, Emmanuelle Charpentier and Jennifer Doudna were awarded the Nobel Prize in Chemistry in 2020.

- Charpentier's research has also contributed to a better understanding of the bacterial immune system and its role in protecting organisms from viral infections.

- She has received numerous other awards and honors in recognition of her scientific contributions and leadership in the field of microbiology and gene editing.

Maryam Mirzakhani

Mathematician

Profile

Date of Birth	May 3, 1977
Place of Birth	Tehran, Iran
Date of Death	July 14, 2017
Nationality	Iranian

Education

Bachelor's degree in Mathematics
Sharif University of Technology in Tehran
1999

Ph.D. in Mathematics
Harvard University
2004

Contributions

- Became the first woman to receive the prestigious Fields Medal in 2014, the highest honor in mathematics, for her exceptional contributions to the fields of geometry and dynamical systems.

- Her groundbreaking research focused on the study of Riemann surfaces and their moduli spaces, shedding new light on the geometry of these complex surfaces and advancing our understanding of their properties.

- Made significant contributions to the theory of Teichmüller dynamics, a field that explores the behavior of complex geometric structures and their deformations.

- Developed new mathematical techniques and approaches that have had a profound impact on various areas of mathematics, including hyperbolic geometry, ergodic theory, and symplectic geometry.

Legacy

Maryam Mirzakhani's work has left an indelible mark on mathematics and has inspired countless mathematicians, particularly women, to pursue careers in the field.

KIZZMEKIA S. CORBETT

Viral Immunologist

PROFILE

○ **Full Name:** Kizzmekia Shanta Corbett

○ **Date of Birth:** January 26, 1986

○ **Place of Birth:** Hurdle Mills, North Carolina, USA

○ **Nationality:** American

EDUCATION

○ **2008** Bachelor of Science (BS) in Biological Sciences, University of Maryland, Baltimore County

○ **2014** Doctor of Philosophy (Ph.D.) in Microbiology and Immunology, University of North Carolina at Chapel Hill

CAREER

2014-present

- Research Fellow, Vaccine Research Center, National Institute of Allergy and Infectious Diseases (NIAID), National Institutes of Health (NIH)
- Key member of the team that developed the mRNA-based Moderna COVID-19 vaccine.
- Conducted groundbreaking research on coronavirus spike proteins and their role in vaccine development.
- Collaborated with multidisciplinary teams to accelerate vaccine response during global health emergencies.

ACHIEVEMENTS

- Received the 2021 Service to America Medal (Sammies) for her contributions to the COVID-19 vaccine development.
- Recognized as one of TIME's 100 Most Influential People in 2020.
- Awarded the North Carolina Order of the Long Leaf Pine for her exceptional achievements in science and public service.

LEGACY AND IMPACT

- Played a pivotal role in the global effort to combat the COVID-19 pandemic through vaccine development.

Printed in Great Britain
by Amazon

34017907R00057